REFLECTING CULTURE:
The Evolution of
American
COMIC BOOK
Super Heroes

FRONT COVER: Background: Fred Ray, original art for the cover of *Action Comics* #50 (DC Comics, July 1942), pen and ink on paper, collection of Joe and Nadia Mannarino STRIP OF SUPERMAN COVERS: Fred Ray, original art for the cover of *Action Comics* #50 (DC Comics, July 1942); Jack Burnley, cover for *Action Comics* #59 (DC Comics, April 1943); Wayne Boring and Stan Kaye, cover for *Action Comics* #101 (DC Comics, October 1946); Al Plastino and Stan Kaye, cover for *Superman* #67 (DC Comics, November/December 1950); Curt Swan and George Klein, cover for *Action Comics* # 357 (DC Comics, December 1967); Curt Swan and Murphy Anderson, cover for *Action Comics* #401 (DC Comics, June 1971); Neal Adams, cover for *Superman* #240 (DC Comics, July 1971); Curt Swan and Murphy Anderson, cover for *Action Comics* #583 (DC Comics, September 1986); Dan Jurgens and Brett Breeding, cover for *Superman* #76 (DC Comics, February 1993); Adam Kubert, original art for the cover of *Action Comics* #844 (DC Comics, December 2006) BACK COVER: Detail from Jack Kirby, Original art for interior page of *Marvel Treasury Special...Featuring Captain America's Bicentennial Battles* (Marvel Comics, 1976), Pen and ink on paper, Collection of Michael Uslan STRIP OF CAPTAIN AMERICA COVERS: Jack Kirby and Joe Simon, cover for *Captain America Comics* #1 (Marvel Comics, April 1941); John Romita, Sr., cover for *Captain America Comics* #78 (Marvel Comics, September 1954); Jack Kirby, cover for *Captain America* #117 (Marvel Comics, September 1969); Greg and Tim Hildebrandt, *Captain America*, 1994, acrylic on board; Steve Epting, cover for *Captain America (Civil War Epilogue)* #25 (April 2007)

Photo credit for original comic art illustrated on covers and pp. 2,4,9,10, 15,17, 19,23,27,31,33, 35,37,46,49,51,52, 53, 56,58,60,61: Peter Jacobs, Montclair, NJ, 2007

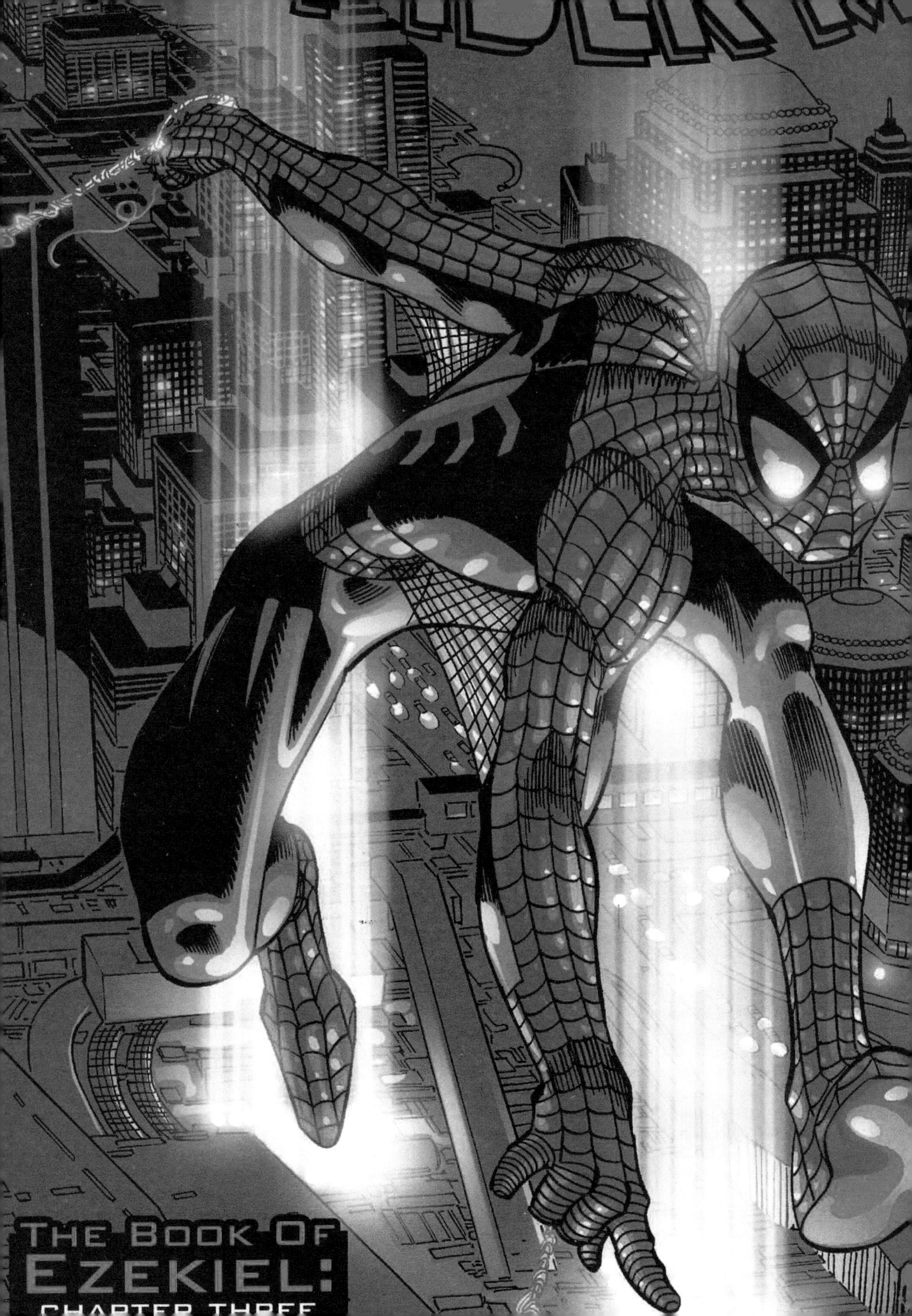
THE BOOK OF
EZEKIEL:
CHAPTER THREE

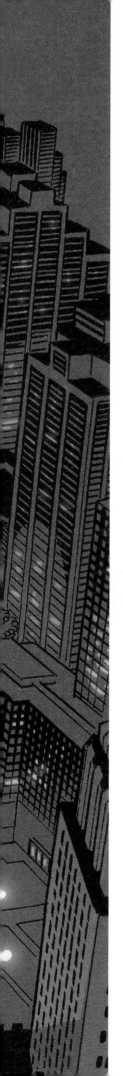

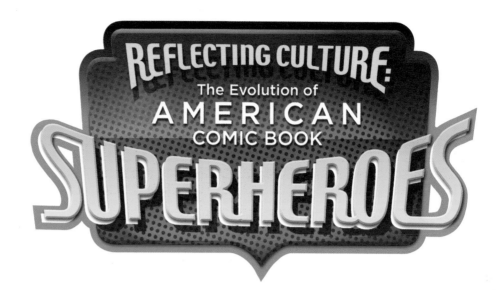

Reflecting Culture: The Evolution of American Comic Book Superheroes

By GAIL STAVITSKY

CONTRIBUTIONS BY:

Michael Uslan

Patterson Sims

Twig Johnson

Detail from: John Romita, Jr., cover artist, ***The Amazing Spider-Man*** #508 (Marvel Comics, July 2004)

ISBN # 978-0-936489-62-9
Library of Congress Control Number 2007935283

Montclair Art Museum
© 2007 Montclair Art Museum
3 South Mountain Avenue
Montclair, NJ 07042 -1747
(973) 746-5555
www.montclairartmuseum.org

Published on the occasion of the exhibition *Reflecting Culture: The Evolution of American Comic Book Super Heroes*, organized by the Montclair Art Museum. July 14, 2007-January 13, 2008

This publication is made possible with generous support from the JPMorgan Chase Foundation, the David and Susan Bershad Foundation and the Judith Targan Endowment Fund for Museum Publications.

MAJOR EXHIBITION FUNDING PROVIDED BY:
The Blanche & Irving Laurie Foundation
NJ Department of State-NJ State Council on the Arts
JPMorgan Chase Foundation
The David & Susan Bershad Foundation

Additional Support Provided By:
The Vance Wall Foundation
The Karma Foundation
Annie sez
Mandee

EXHIBITION ANGELS
Bobbi Brown & Steven Plofker
Rose & John Cali
Paula Tuffin & Reg Hollinger
Carol & Harlan Waksal
Margo & Frank Walter
Joan & Donald Zief

The Judith Targan Endowment Fund for Museum Publications
Jacqueline McMullen

This exhibition was selected by the New Jersey State Council on the Arts as part of the American Masterpieces Series in New Jersey. American Masterpieces is a program of the National Endowment for the Arts. All Museum programs are made possible, in part, by the New Jersey State Council on the Arts/Department of State, a Partner Agency of the National Endowment for the Arts and by funds from the National Endowment for the Arts; the Geraldine R. Dodge Foundation; and Museum members.

DESIGNED BY: Rich Sheinaus, Gotham Design, NYC
PRINTED BY: Friesens Press

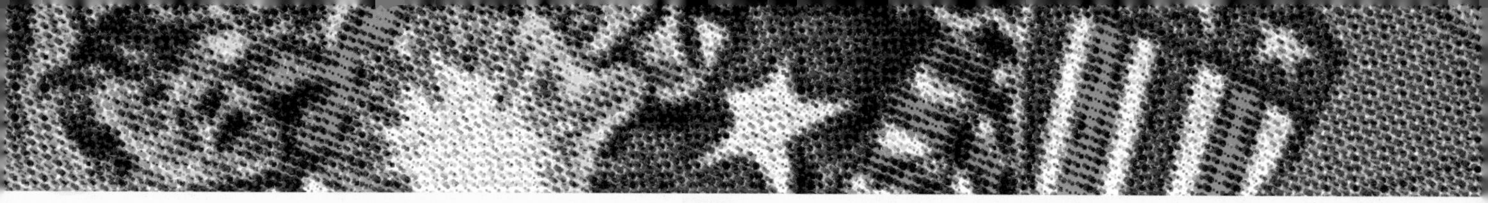

Table of Contents

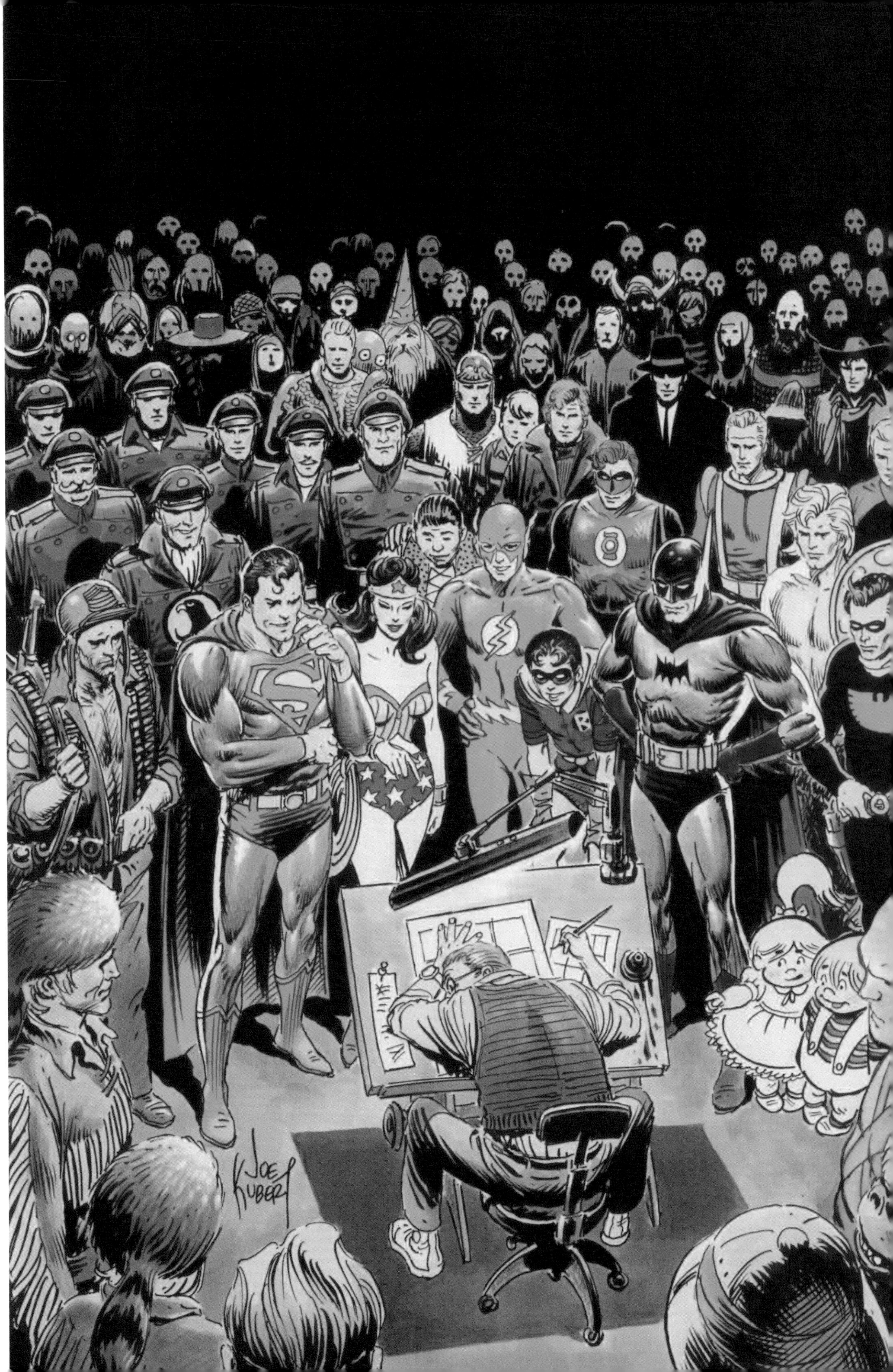
JOE KUBERT

DIRECTOR'S FOREWORD & ACKNOWLEDGEMENTS
By PATTERSON SIMS

Two years ago I learned from Susan Bershad, a trustee of the Montclair Art Museum, of the existence of a Montclair-area collection of rare, historically important comic books owned by Michael Uslan, the executive producer of the *Batman* films. With the recent success of the Museum-organized exhibitions, **Roy Lichtenstein: American Indian Encounters** and **Anxious Objects: Willie Cole's Favorite Brands**, the Board of Trustees and the staff had been discussing ways to include aspects of popular culture more directly into the Museum's program. The Lichtenstein and Cole shows had addressed potent social and cultural issues. The esteemed Pop artist Lichtenstein found inspiration from comics, cartoons, and mass culture, and Willie Cole deploys everyday consumer objects as his artistic media. Yet a show that actually focused on popular culture had not yet been presented by the Museum.

Seeing is believing; immediately upon visiting the Uslan collection, the Museum's curators Gail Stavitsky and Twig Johnson and I were convinced of the American comic book's artistry and potential for an exhibition at the Museum. The unique capacity of comic books to merge text, pictures, and storytelling to address popular culture, mythology, and the powerful role of super heroes makes them the perfect means to offer an exhibition of the highest quality and broadest public appeal. In a period when numerous contemporary visual artists have embraced the smaller scale of drawing and its illustrative powers and used words as primary artistic media, comic books seemed—not only for their inspiration of art—worthy in their own right to be the subject of an art exhibition. The accessibility and fascination that comic books elicit offered the Museum an unparalleled opportunity to attract, engage, and inform a wider audience. Michael Chabon's potent novel *The Amazing Adventures of Kavalier & Clay*, the success of the spate of recent *X-Men*, *Batman*, *Spider-Man* comic book-based movies and cult films like *Crumb* and *American Splendor* demonstrate the breadth of adult fascination with the American comic book and broad veneration of the medium's inspiring and now legendary creators, characters, and super heroes.

Uslan's holdings and his infectious enthusiasm, extensive knowledge, and numerous contacts quickly elevated an idea into an exhibition. Stavitsky and Johnson realized the power of bringing together comic books and the original comic artwork. Stavitsky's prior, personal interest in and knowledge about comic books predisposed her to the allure and influence of the medium. She saw comic books as a reflection of culture and society and the shifting roles and identities of these valiant protagonists in the struggle of good and evil. Stavitsky has used her formidable scholarly skills and curatorial gifts to make the evolution, power, and meaning of comic books lucid and artful, She wisely emphasized original drawings to make the fantastic graphic skill of the two-part drawing process abundantly apparent.

JOE KUBERT
Original art for the cover of THE GREATEST HEROES OF THE 1950s (DC Comics, 1990)
Watercolor on paper
Collection of Joe Kubert

Reflecting Culture: The Evolution of American Comic Book Super Heroes soon begat three complementary, smaller exhibitions; **Comic Book Legends: Joe, Adam, and Andy Kubert**; **Greg Hildebrandt: Golden and Silver Age Super Heroes**; and **Dulce Pinzón: The Real Story of the Super Heroes**. We also are gratified that a documentary film has been made by Montclair-based Stonebridge Productions, LLC, produced and directed by noted

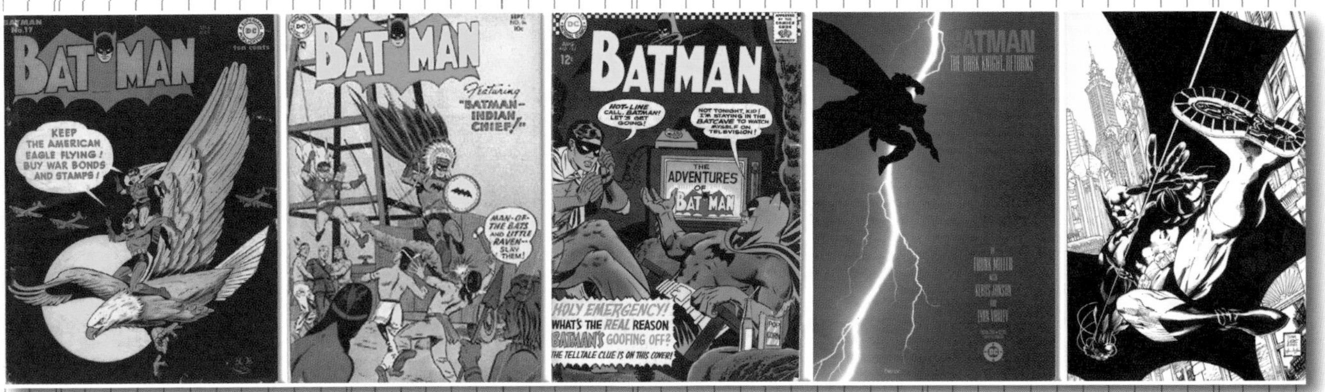
BATMAN
KEEP THE AMERICAN EAGLE FLYING! BUY WAR BONDS AND STAMPS!
BATMAN
Featuring "BATMAN—INDIAN CHIEF!"
MAN-OF-THE BATS AND LITTLE RAVEN— SLAY THEM!
BATMAN
12¢
HOT-LINE CALL, BATMAN! LET'S GET GOING!
NOT TONIGHT, KID! I'M STAYING IN THE BATCAVE TO WATCH MYSELF ON TELEVISION!
THE ADVENTURES OF BATMAN
HOLY EMERGENCY!
WHAT'S THE REAL REASON BATMAN'S GOOFING OFF?
THE TELLTALE CLUE IS ON THIS COVER!

Jerry Robinson, cover for *Batman* #17 (DC Comics, June/July 1943); J. Winslow Mortimer, cover for *Batman* #86 (DC Comics, September 1955); Carmine Infantino and Murphy Anderson, cover for *Batman* #183 (DC Comics, August 1966); Frank Miller and Klaus Janson, cover for *Batman: The Dark Knight Returns Book One* (DC Comics, 1986); Jim Lee and Scott Williams, original art for the cover of *Batman* #608 (December 2002)

filmmaker Chip Cronkite, with Executive Producer Michael Uslan, and Associate Producer Jacqueline Knox. This film project preserves the reminiscences of the pioneering comic book artists and creators who are still with us today. It will include highlights of the exhibition and provide curatorial insights. The New Jersey connections of many of the creators of comic books became a further substantiation of the aptness of this subject for the Montclair Art Museum.

Twig Johnson initiated and oversaw the exhibition's commitment to Native American and multi-cultural expression. The Museum's Director of Operations, Carlos Gálvez, and his wife, Dr. Alyshia F. Gálvez, Assistant Professor/Faculty Fellow of Latin American and Caribbean Studies, New York University, introduced Dulce Pinzón's photographs of everyday super heroes to the Museum. Their sociological power and metaphors repositioned our perception of a super hero. The curators and the Museum's Education Department saw the didactic value of comic books and their high educational value for literacy and role modeling. Public education programs held during the show will bring other leading scholars and some of the legendary comic book artists themselves to the Museum. The creation of an innovative Family Learning Lab, where children can transform themselves into the super hero of their own choice or imagination, work on art-making projects with adults, and be photographed with super hero figures, is another first-time and innovative educational aspect for this show. The exhibitions will also feature the first-ever MAM audio tour using the visitors' own and lent mobile phones to access commentaries by Michael Uslan, the curators, and some of the comic book artists.

Starting with Susan Bershad and Michael and Nancy Uslan, this project has engaged tremendous individual support and commitment. Its merits, and Uslan's persuasive eloquence, have elicited generous project funding. Having been the key funder of ***Roy Lichtenstein: American Indian Encounters*** and made a substantial gift for the Museum's expansion that made the Blanche and Irving Laurie Foundation Art Stairway (where Greg Hildebrandt's ***Golden and Silver Age Super Heroes*** murals are being shown), the Museum's generous friends at the Blanche and Irving Laurie Foundation provided the lead and largest gift for ***Reflecting Culture: The Evolution of American Comic Book Super Heroes***. We owe special thanks to Gene R. Korf and Scott Korf of the Laurie Foundation for their instant ability to see the potential for this show.

The project is supported by a major grant from the NJ Department of State–NJ State Council on the Arts. The exhibition was selected by the New Jersey State Council on the Arts as part of the American Masterpieces Series in New Jersey. American Masterpieces is a program of the National Endowment for the Arts. The JPMorgan Chase Foundation provided record-breaking corporate support for the show's many special education initiatives. Major individual leadership support for this show and its related publication has come from the Susan and David Bershad Foundation.

For several years, the Museum's increasingly ambitious exhibition projects have been funded by Exhibition Angels, generous Museum supporters who give a minimum of $10,000 to help cover the costs of exhibitions. Exhibition Angels for this show include Bobbi Brown and Steven Plofker, Rose and John Cali, Paula Tuffin and Reg Hollinger, Carol and Harlan Waksal, Margo and Frank Walter and Joan and Donald Zief. Additional support has been provided by The Karma Foundation, Vance Wall Foundation, Annie sez and Mandee, and funds from the Museum's Judith Targan Endowment Fund for Museum Publications helped underwrite this publication. Other major contributions to this project have been made by Peter and Dottie Frank and other members of the Board of Trustees Gretchen Prater and Lynn Glasser, for hosting and underwriting the opening dinner. Mort and Patricia David donated the Superman sculpture that welcomes visitors to the show, and Jacqueline McMullen has helped underwrite other project costs.

To gain the endorsement and approval for the use of images from DC and Marvel, the leading comic book publishers, was absolutely crucial to the success of this catalogue. We are therefore especially grateful to DC's staff, starting with Paul Levitz, President and Publisher, as well as Thomas King, Rights Administrator, Steve Korte, Group Editor, Licensed Publishing, Barbara Rich, Director of Licensing, David Hyde, Director of Publicity, Joel Press, Manager, Business Affairs, Paula Lowitt, Senior VP, Business and Legal Affairs, and Lillian Laserson, Senior Counsel. At Marvel Comics, we thank Dan Buckley, President & Publisher; Carol G. Pinkus, Director, Intellectual Property; and, Chris Allo, Editorial Talent Coordinator, for their willingness to permit the Museum to use images in this accompanying publication. We also greatly appreciate the pro-bono legal assistance of Alan Lewis and Barry Ageeren as we addressed copyright issues that have never confronted the Museum previously.

Many others, as acknowledged by Gail Stavitsky, contributed to the successful realization of this unique exhibition and its accompanying catalogue and programs. We are grateful for the special support for print media placement provided by Nanette Leonard, Public Relations. On behalf of the Staff and the Museum's Board of Trustees, gratitude is expressed to all the numerous donors, Trustees, and staff members who have worked together to allow the Montclair Art Museum to be the first art museum to document and explore the evolution, political and social history, and aesthetic impact of comic books from 1938 to the present.

CURATOR'S INTRODUCTION & ACKNOWLEDGEMENTS
By GAIL STAVITSKY

> *From the 1930s through today, comic books have*
> *expressed the trends, conventions, and concerns of American life...*
> *Comics have been a showcase for national views, slang,*
> *morals, customs, traditions, racial attitudes, fads,*
> *heroes of the day, and everything else that makes up our lifestyles.*
> *– Michael Uslan, The Comic Book Revolution (1977)*

The modern comic book, from its humble origins in
1934 as the reprinted pages of Sunday newspaper comic strips,
quickly grew into a thriving industry that at that time became the most
popular producer of reading material for children and young adults. This
dramatic growth was fuelled by the proliferation of the new super hero comic book
characters who appeared in the era of the Great Depression and World War II. Like the
mythological heroes of ancient Greece, the comic book super heroes became manifestations
of American history, culture, and folklore. As Michael Uslan, executive producer of *Batman*
and *Batman Begins*, has observed, "the ancient gods of the Greeks, Romans, the Egyptians,
and the Norse still exist today, only they're clad in spandex, capes, and masks."

The exhibition **Reflecting Culture: The Evolution of American Comic Book Super
Heroes** traces the way in which comic books have reflected national events, aspirations,
and attitudes–from the battles waged against Axis powers and corporate corruption by the
invincible Superman, Batman, and Captain America, to the era of the 1960s when Spider-
Man emerged as the quintessential super hero of his time–an adolescent who had to
contend with his own insecurities while fighting evil. This reworking of the formulas for
super heroes was also evidenced by greater diversity in comic books with the introduction
of African American, Native American, and other minority characters. The exhibition
concludes with an open-ended section exploring the impact of the 9-11 crisis as super
heroes of the new century worked alongside real, ordinary heroes to address the greatest
catastrophe on American soil.

This project began with an important introduction to the world of comic books at the
behest of Museum board member Susan Bershad. During various discussions devoted to
strategic planning, Susan rightly observed that an exhibition devoted to popular culture
would attract new audiences for the Museum. Fairly soon thereafter, she introduced
Montclair Art Museum Director Patterson Sims, Twig Johnson, Curator of Native American
Art, and myself to Michael Uslan. Little did we know that the award-winning Executive
Producer of *Batman Begins* (2005) lived right in our own neighborhood and was responsible
for teaching the first college level comic book course at his alma mater Indiana University!

Michael has recalled that "the idea of this whole comic book exhibition was actually
hatched by Susan Bershad and my wife, Nancy, who knew I've been looking for a way to
give back to our local community and suggested to me that this would be the perfect way."

Michael immediately dedicated himself to the execution and promotion of this project, serving as primary consultant on all aspects. Through many discussions, he played a critical role in shaping the unique direction of this exhibition, which is the first to examine the history of mainstream comic books from a social history perspective, in combination with a presentation of original comic art that emphasizes the aesthetic qualities of this uniquely American art form. There are many historical works on display in this show that have never been publicly on display in a museum.

Michael has contributed an insightful essay to this catalogue, building upon his own prolific writings. His thesis *The Comic Book Revolution* (1977) was very helpful with the conceptualization of this exhibition, as were his many introductions to his colleagues. Furthermore, Michael's own excellent and diverse collection served as the foundation for the initial loans for the exhibition. Through Michael, I met Joe and Nadia Mannarino of All Star Auctions **(www.allstarauc.com)**, leaders in the field of comic character collectibles for over 25 years and the primary resource for original comic art, comic books and professional appraisals. Joe and Nadia very generously agreed to lend works from their own superb collection of original comic art and have provided greatly appreciated guidance and support throughout the planning of this show. Joe and Nadia patiently shared their phenomenal expertise and, in addition, posted my requests for specific comics and comic art, which resulted in critical contacts with many other lenders to the show.

I would like to extend a special thank you to Stephen Fishler, Vincent Zurzolo and Ben Smith of Metropolis Collectibles, NYC, which offers the world's largest selection of Golden, Silver and Bronze Age comic books (1938-1980) on its website, **www.MetropolisComics.com**. They very generously agreed to lend many of the comic books in this show, as well as major examples of original comic art from Stephen Fishler's outstanding private collection. My additional thanks go to **www.GothamCityArt.com** for its own contributions to the exhibit.

Another major lender to the show is Srihari S. Naidu, M.D., who has also been very generous in sharing his enthusiasm and knowledge of the field, personally introducing me to dealers and collectors at the New York Comic Con in February 2007. Other lenders who were particularly magnanimous include Daniel Herman, Ankur Jetley, Michigan State University Libraries (a treasure trove of comics for which Randall W. Scott, Special Division was especially helpful), Win Murray, Eric Roberts, Ethan Roberts, and Scott Webb. Jim Halperin and Greg Holman of Heritage Auction Galleries (**HA.com**) very generously lent a number of their important comic books. Among the other lenders to the show are various leading artists in the field: Amanda Conner, Denys Cowan, Greg Hildebrandt, Steve McNiven, Scott Williams, as well as Joe, Adam, and Andy Kubert. Several of these artists are from New Jersey and are the subjects of two concurrent exhibitions: *Comic Book Legends: Joe, Adam, and Andy Kubert* and *Greg Hildebrandt: Golden and Silver Age Super Heroes*.

We recognize the invaluable participation of the following living legends of the comic book art form in the documentary film project of Stonebridge Productions, LLC, with Chip Cronkite, Producer and Director, Michael Uslan, Executive Producer, and Jacqueline Knox, Associate

Producer: Murphy Anderson, Allen Bellman, Ramona Fradon, Dick Giordano, Irwin Hasen, Greg Hildebrandt, Sheldon Moldoff, Joe Kubert, Adam Kubert, Andy Kubert, Stan Lee, Denny O'Neil, Jerry Robinson, John Romita, Sr., Lew Sayer Schwartz, Joe Simon, and Roy Thomas.

Reflecting Culture: The Evolution of American Comic Book Super Heroes would not have been possible without the very generous participation of all the lenders who are listed on the Lenders page in this catalogue. The special presentation of the documentary *Comic Book Super Heroes Unmasked* (2003) was made possible courtesy of The History Channel; special thanks to Libby O'Connell and Cara Tocci for granting permission and providing a screening copy of the DVD. Others who helped with the realization of this show include Jean Scrocco, Pete Carlsson, Missy Sullivan, Steve Borock, Evan Burse, Adam McGovern, Spencer Beck, Peter Coogan, Jimmy Palmiotti, and Susan Yoon, Executive Director of Development and External Relations at Indiana University Libraries, which houses a significant collection of comic books donated by Michael Uslan. An exhibition of these comic books at Indiana University's Lilly Library was helpful in the formative stages of this project.

Many Museum staff members played important roles in the realization of this project. Twig Johnson was especially helpful both in the determination of the focus of the show and in its various planning stages. Her sound advice, support, and collegiality are always greatly appreciated. In her organization of the section devoted to American Indian super heroes, Twig was vitally assisted by Rob Schmidt, creator of the *Peace Party* comics and a leading comic book expert on Native themes in comics. Through his efforts, the Montclair Art Museum's Le Brun Library now has a collection of 138 comic books that show the evolution of American Indian characters from stereotypical depictions to present-day tribally created and produced comic books that celebrate native cultures and beliefs. Twig and I attended Rob's inspiring panel discussion at the Eiteljorg Museum of American Indians and Western Art with leading native creators Michael Sheyahshe (*Caddo*) and his soon to be released book *Native Americans in Comic Books*, Steven Keewatin Sanderson, author and artist for *The Healthy Aboriginal Network* comic book *Darkness Calls*, and writer Richard Van Camp (Dogrib).

Other members of the Museum's curatorial department played key roles in the implementation of this project. Associate Registrar Erica Boyd, with the assistance of Registrar Renée Powley, skillfully assumed the daunting task of the loans process and arranging for the safe transport of the myriad works of art in the show. Head Preparator and Exhibits Designer Bruce Rainier and Jason Van Yperen, Preparator handled all aspects of the stunning installation of this exhibition. Danielle Labbate, Curatorial Assistant, provided clerical, registrarial, and research support.

Aran Roche, Director of Grants and fundraiser extraordinaire, worked very hard to arrange for the financial support for this exhibition. Beth Hart, Director of Individual Giving was also very helpful. Jennifer Strikowsky, Director of Marketing and Communications and Toni Liquori, former Media Relations Manager, with the assistance of Charlotte Howard, Design Manager and John Adams, Education Administrative Assistant, coordinated all publicity outreach and printed materials, including the publication of this catalogue. Gary Schneider,

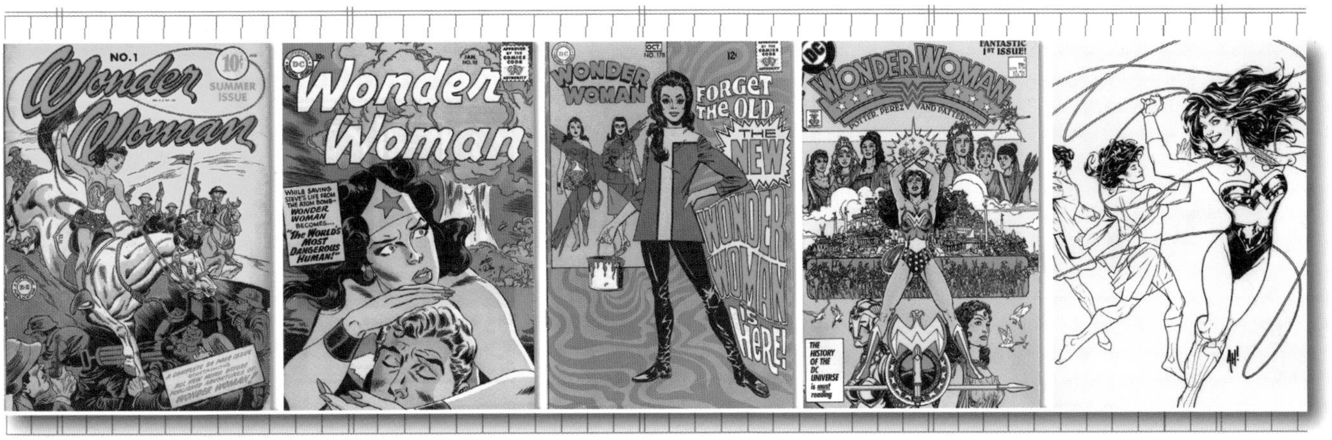
NO. 1
SUMMER ISSUE
Wonder Woman
Wonder Woman
WONDER WOMAN
FORGET THE OLD
THE NEW
WONDER WOMAN IS HERE!
FANTASTIC 1ST ISSUE!
WONDER WOMAN

Harry G. Peter, cover for *Wonder Woman* #1 (DC Comics, Summer 1942); Ross Andru and Mike Esposito, cover for *Wonder Woman* #95 (DC Comics, January 1958); Mike Sekowsky and Dick Giordano, cover for *Wonder Woman* #178 (DC Comics, September-October 1968); George Perez, cover for *Wonder Woman* Vol. 2, #1 (DC Comics, February 1987); Original art by Adam Hughes for the cover of *Wonder Woman: The Ultimate Guide to the Amazon Princess* (Dorling Kindersley, 2003)

Director of Education, Pia Cooperman, former Public Programs Coordinator, and Abby McBride, Coordinator for School Programs and Tours were responsible for the educational programming and Family Learning Lab, and also the direction of the audio guide and Comic Book Family Guide, written by R. S. Paulette and drawn by Reilly Brown, Jason Baroody, Aaron Kuder, Khoi Pham, and Chris Burnham of Ten Ton Studios, a coalition of artists and writers.

I would also like to thank Rich Sheinaus of Gotham Design for the superlative design of this catalogue and the exhibition graphics. Rich also shared his considerable comic book expertise and served as a generous lender to the show.

LENDERS to the EXHIBITION

Alan Bartholomew
Jon Berk
Steve Carey
Amanda Conner
Denys Cowan
Dan Cusimano
Chris Eberle, WildPig Comics II
Stephen Fishler, President of MetropolisComics.com
P.C. Hamerlinck
Heritage Auction Galleries
Daniel and Louise Herman
Greg Hildebrandt and Jean Scrocco, Spiderweb Art, Inc.
Ankur and Indu Jetley
Joe Kubert
Adam Kubert
Andy Kubert
Joseph P. Latino
Le Brun Library, Montclair Art Museum
Steven Lee
Paul Leggett
Dan Makara
Joe and Nadia Mannarino
Steve McNiven
MetropolisComics.com
Michigan State University Libraries
Win Murray
Srihari S. Naidu, M.D.
Eric Roberts
Ethan Roberts
Rich Sheinaus
Ben Smith, MetropolisComics.com and GothamCityArt.com
Maggie Thompson
Michael Uslan
Joseph Veteri
Scott Webb
Scott Williams

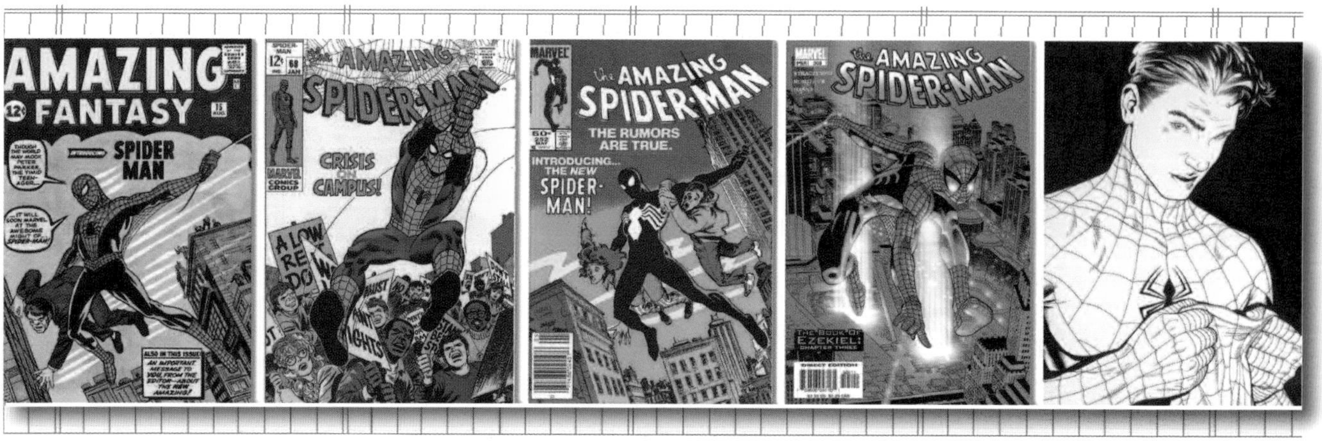
AMAZING FANTASY
SPIDER MAN
THE AMAZING SPIDER-MAN
CRISIS ON CAMPUS!
THE AMAZING SPIDER-MAN
THE RUMORS ARE TRUE.
INTRODUCING... THE NEW SPIDER-MAN!
THE AMAZING SPIDER-MAN

Jack Kirby and Steve Ditko, cover for *Amazing Fantasy* #15 (Marvel Comics, August 1962); John Romita, Sr., cover for *The Amazing Spider-Man* #68 (Marvel Comics, January 1969); Ron Frenz and Klaus Janson, cover for *The Amazing Spider-Man* #252 (Marvel Comics, May 1984); John Romita, Jr., cover for *The Amazing Spider-Man* #508 (Marvel Comics, July 2004); Steve McNiven, Original art for interior page of *Civil War* #2 (Marvel Comics, August 2006)

STATEMENT

Thirty-five years ago, I began teaching the world's first accredited college course on comic books at Indiana University. My course premise was based on three concepts I believed in with my heart and soul, but the rest of the world refused to acknowledge: comic books are a legitimate art form as indigenous to America as jazz; comic books have, over the decades, been sociological reflectors of a changing American culture; and comic books are contemporary American folklore, with the super-heroes and super-villains being our modern day mythological gods and demons.

To those who scoffed at comic books as art, exhibitions at The Louvre and The Lilly Library, symposiums at The Smithsonian Institution, and the influence of comic books on artists such as Roy Lichtenstein and Andy Warhol, validates my thirty-five year battle for their legitimacy.

To those who doubted the importance of the role of comics as reflectors of our evolving politics, fads, jargon, prejudices, and character, I need only point out how the Asian super-villain in the history of comics has been transformed from the mystic Fu Manchu type of the 1930's, to the blood-drooling and fanged Japanese soldier of the 1940's, to the red barbarian of Asia in the 1950's, to the Viet Cong guerrilla of the 1960's, to the mystic sensei and kung fu master of the 1970's and beyond.

To those who perceived comic books as cheap entertainment for children and refused to accept them as contemporary folklore, I can only recount the story of Moses. The Hebrew people were being persecuted and their first born slain. Determined to save their son, a Hebrew couple places their infant in a little wicker basket and sends him down the River Nile where he's found by an Egyptian couple who raise him as their own son. When he grows up and learns of his true heritage, he becomes a great hero to his people and a champion of their cause. Is there a more recent tale that echoes this story? Yes, there is. A scientist and his wife learn that their planet, Krypton, is about to explode. Determined to save their son, they place their infant in a little rocket ship and send him to Earth where he's found by the Kents who raise him as their own son. When he grows up and learns of his true heritage, he becomes... well...Superman.

The Montclair Art Museum's seminal exhibit, ***Reflecting Culture: The Evolution of American Comic Book Super Heroes***, is essential to society's formal recognition of the art form and its long relevance to the culture. At last, there is an important exhibition dedicated solely to comic books rather than one more show presenting them merely in a shared spotlight with comic strips, pulp magazines, Big Little Books, underground comix, or movie/TV/animated incarnations of the super heroes.

The comic book was born in the early 1930's in New York City. It has finally come of age in 2007 in Montclair, New Jersey.

– Michael Uslan, Exhibition Consultant and Lender

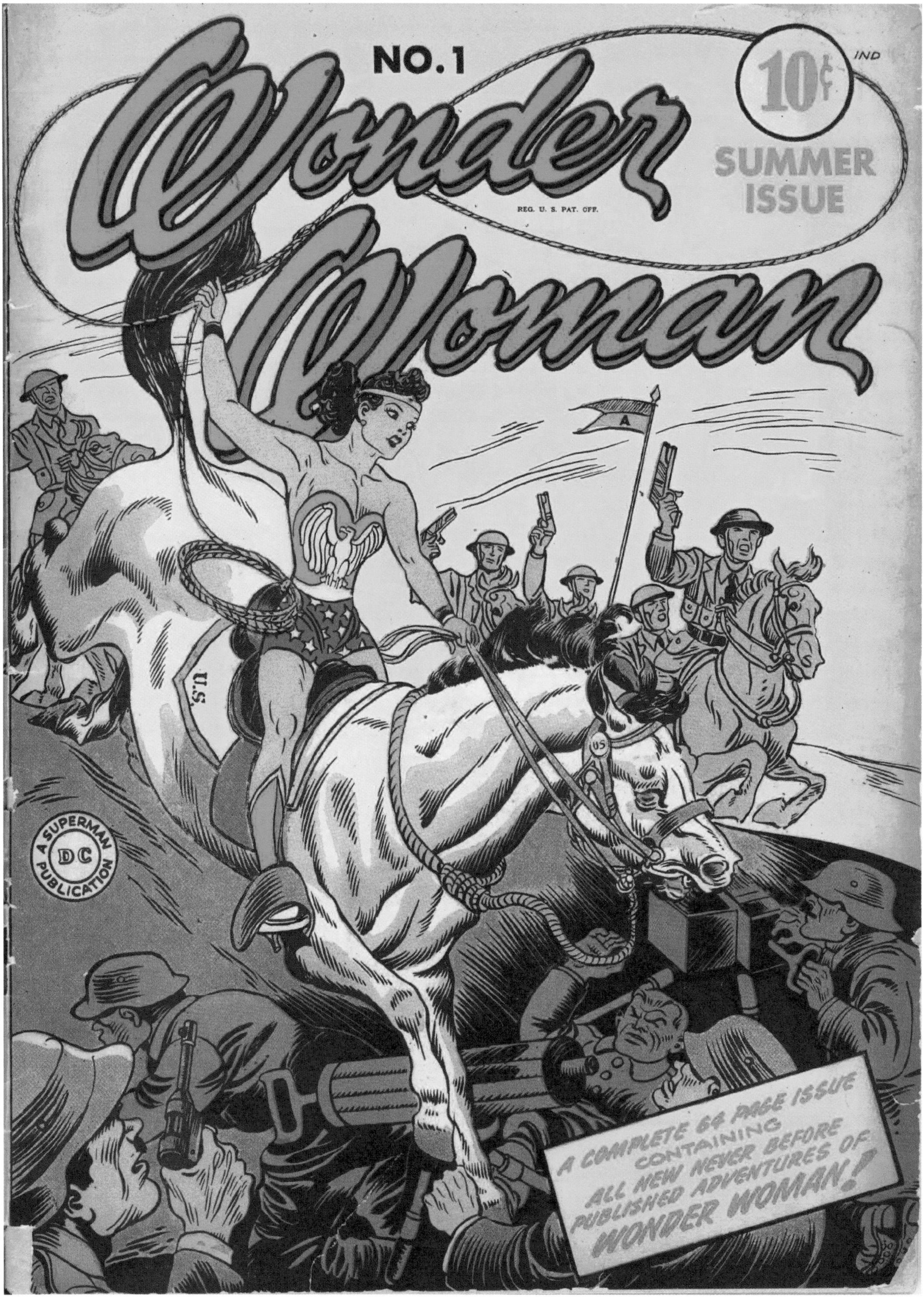
NO. 1
Wonder Woman
REG. U. S. PAT. OFF.
10¢
IND
SUMMER ISSUE
U.S.
US
A SUPERMAN DC PUBLICATION
A COMPLETE 64 PAGE ISSUE CONTAINING ALL NEW NEVER BEFORE PUBLISHED ADVENTURES OF WONDER WOMAN!

SUPER HEROES GO TO WAR:
THE DEPRESSION & NEW DEAL 1938-1945

With the introduction of Superman in *Action Comics* #1 in June 1938, the super hero genre was established as the dominant form of comic book storytelling in what became known as the Golden Age of comics (1938-1946). Writer Jerry Siegel and artist Joe Shuster created Superman as an archetypal character who was, in their words, "A genius in intellect—A Hercules in strength—A Nemesis to wrongdoers!" Superman's dual identity as the all powerful super hero and mild-mannered reporter Clark Kent derived from the adolescent, masculine wish-fulfillment fantasies of his creators, fascinated with such double life avengers as the Scarlet Pimpernel and Zorro. The latter character in the movie *Mark of Zorro* also served as a prototype for Superman's costume, as did the outfits of the circus strongmen of the day. His super-strength was rooted in such 20th century characters as Tarzan and Popeye the Sailor.

Superman's unique identity as an all powerful alien from another planet, Krypton, also established him as an immigrant and thus part of the American dream/myth. His main role, however, during this era was that of champion of the oppressed, a progressive super-reformer aligned against the forces of corporate and government greed to serve the public welfare. He was soon followed by The Batman (*Detective Comics* #27 May 1939), a darker, vigilante crime-fighter who relies on his own scientific knowledge, detective skills, and superior athletic abilities, rather than superhuman powers.

As international conflicts loomed ever larger during this era, the conflict resolution role of super heroes soon expanded into the international arena. Months before the United States entered World War II, American comic book super heroes began fighting the Axis enemies, as seen on the cover of *Captain America Comics* #1 (March 1941) where the definitive patriot slugs Hitler. He was joined by Green Lantern, Captain Marvel, and the first female super hero, Wonder Woman (launched in 1941). Many of the young artists creating these propagandistic comic books were liberal Jews expressing their politics of moral revulsion in their work (i.e. Joe Simon and Jack Kirby, co-creators of Captain America).

AT LEFT

HARRY G. PETER, cover artist
WONDER WOMAN #1 (DC Comics, Summer 1942)
Collection of Michigan State University Libraries

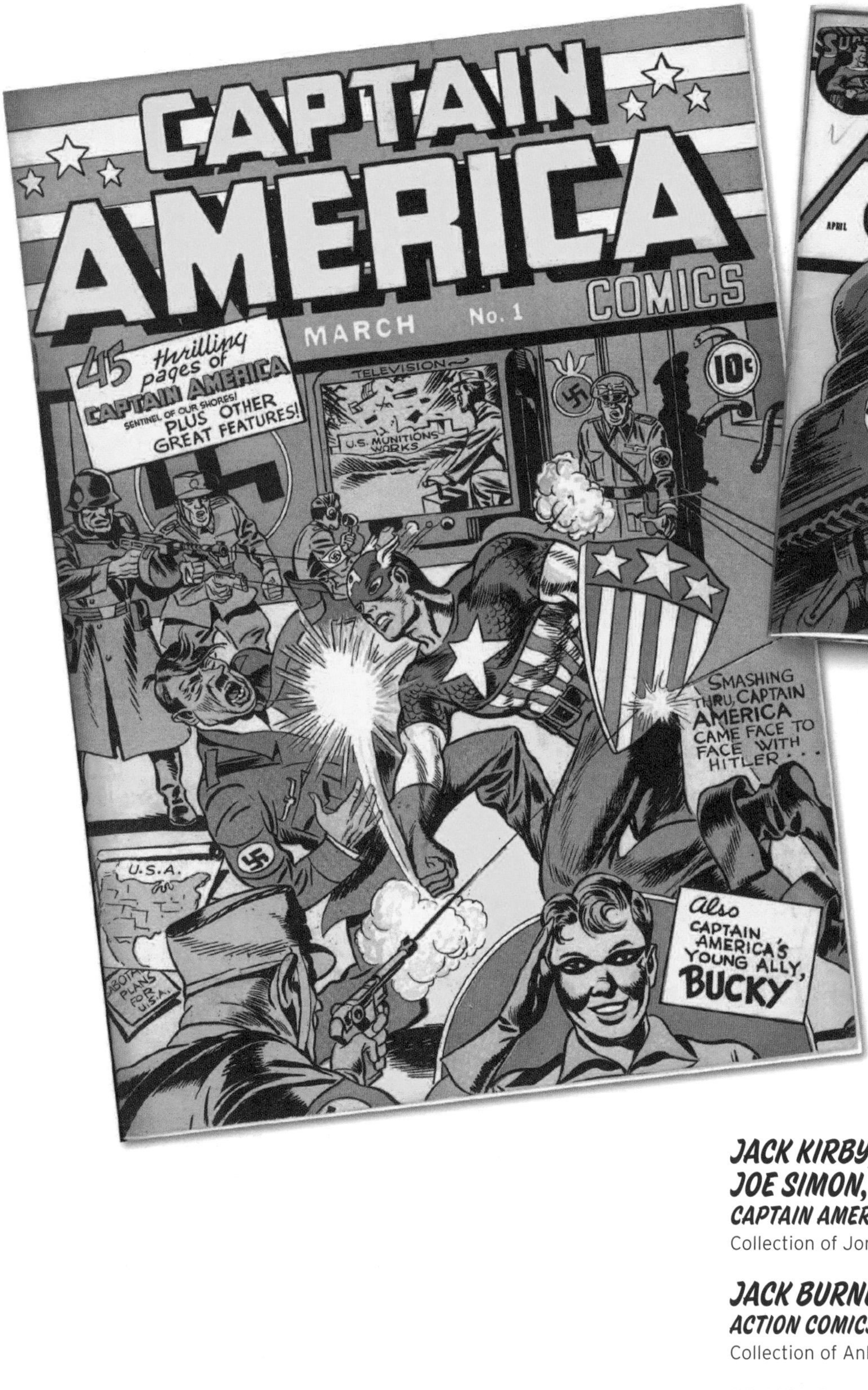
CAPTAIN AMERICA COMICS
MARCH No. 1
10¢
45 thrilling pages of CAPTAIN AMERICA SENTINEL OF OUR SHORES! PLUS OTHER GREAT FEATURES!
TELEVISION
U.S. MUNITIONS WORKS
SMASHING THRU, CAPTAIN AMERICA CAME FACE TO FACE WITH HITLER...
U.S.A.
SABOTAGE PLANS FOR U.S.A.
Also CAPTAIN AMERICA'S YOUNG ALLY, BUCKY

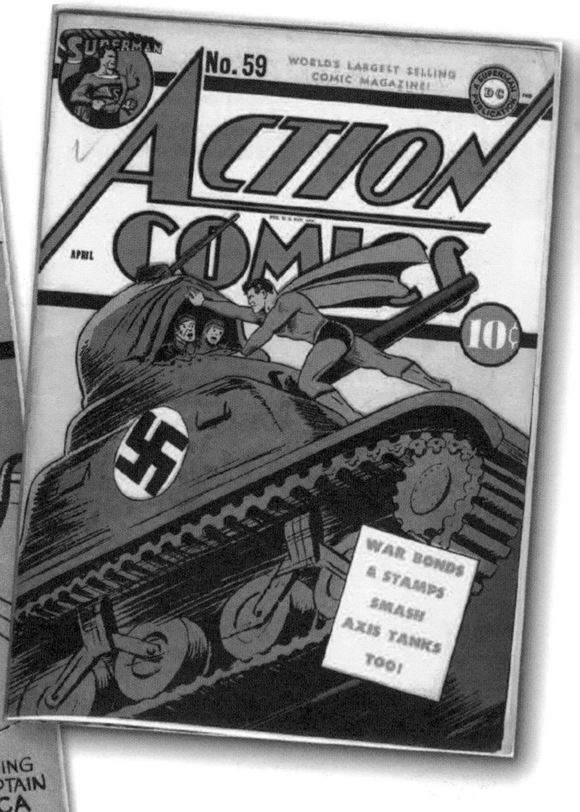
SUPERMAN
No. 59
WORLD'S LARGEST SELLING COMIC MAGAZINE!
ACTION COMICS
APRIL
10¢
WAR BONDS & STAMPS SMASH AXIS TANKS TOO!

JACK KIRBY, cover penciller and
JOE SIMON, cover inker
CAPTAIN AMERICA COMICS #1 (Marvel Comics, March 1941)
Collection of Jon Berk

JACK BURNLEY, cover artist
ACTION COMICS #59 (DC Comics, April 1943)
Collection of Ankur and Indu Jetley

AT RIGHT:

FRED RAY
Original art for the cover of ACTION COMICS #50 (DC Comics, July 1942)
Pen and ink on paper
Collection of Joe and Nadia Mannarino

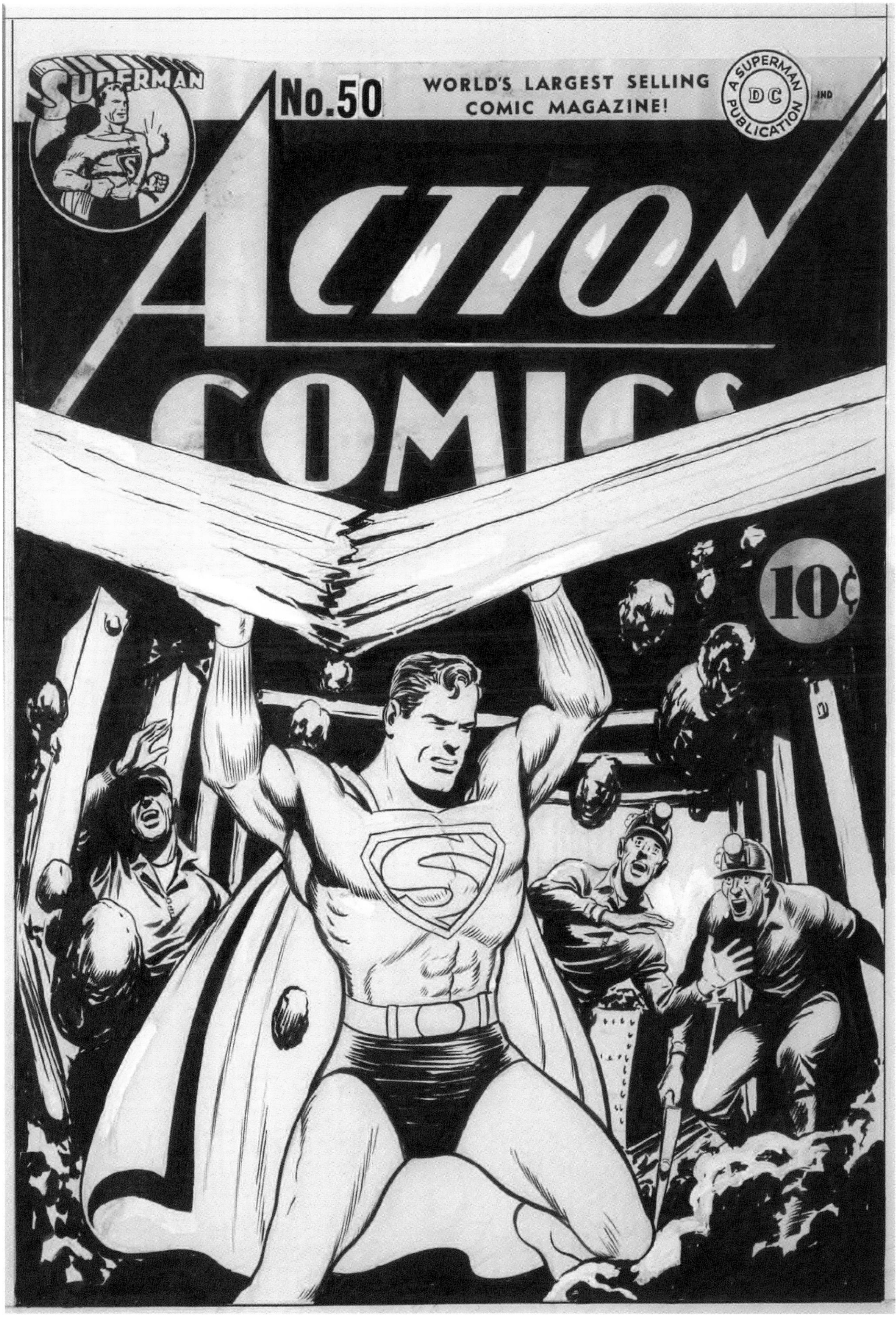
SUPERMAN
No.50
WORLD'S LARGEST SELLING
COMIC MAGAZINE!
A SUPERMAN DC PUBLICATION
IND
ACTION COMICS
10¢

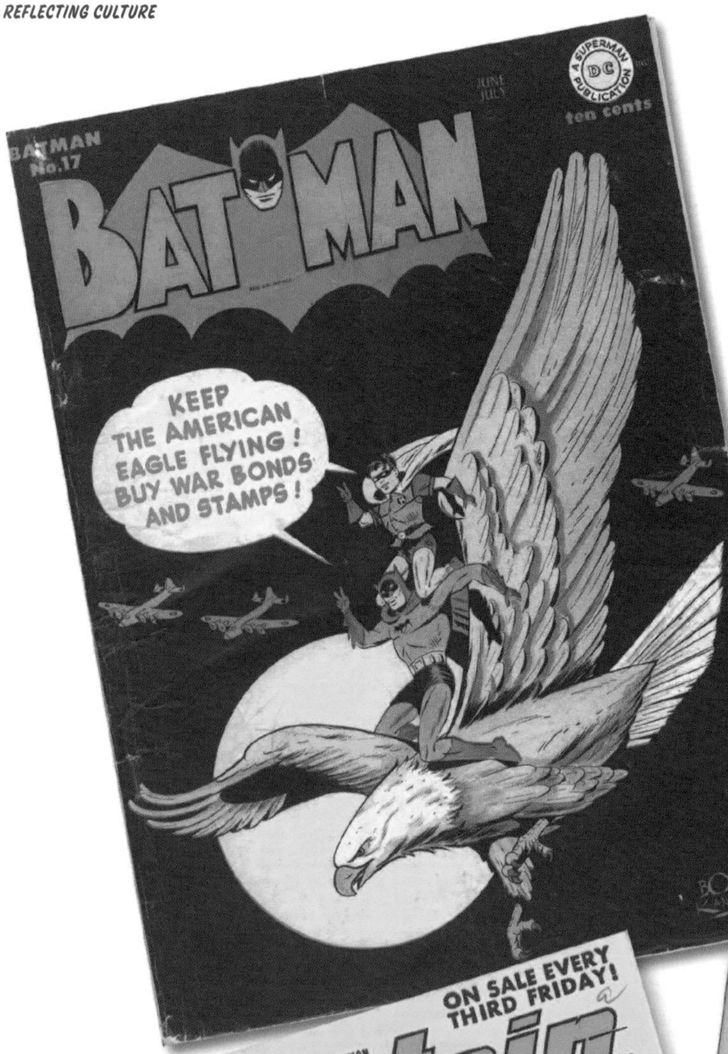
BATMAN
No.17
JUNE
JULY
A SUPERMAN DC PUBLICATION
ten cents
BATMAN
KEEP THE AMERICAN EAGLE FLYING! BUY WAR BONDS AND STAMPS!

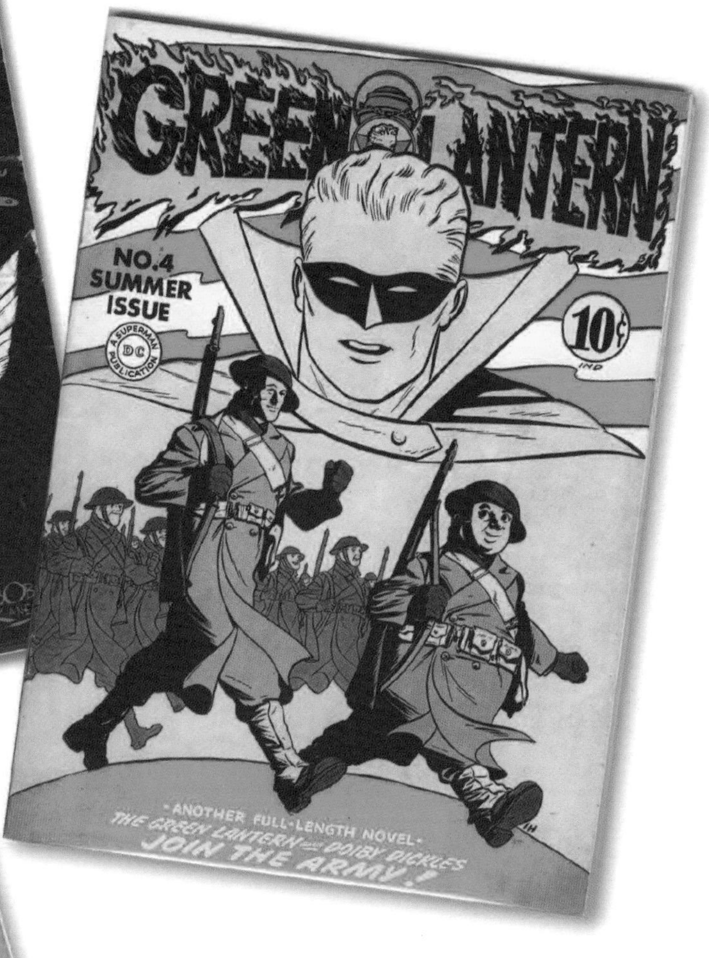
GREEN LANTERN
NO.4 SUMMER ISSUE
A SUPERMAN DC PUBLICATION
10¢
ANOTHER FULL-LENGTH NOVEL
THE GREEN LANTERN and DOIBY DICKLES
JOIN THE ARMY!

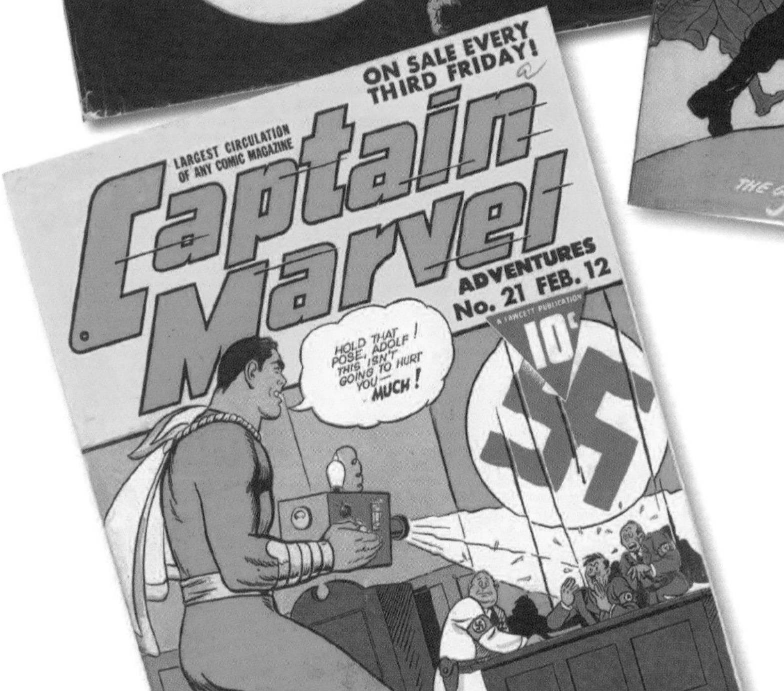
ON SALE EVERY THIRD FRIDAY!
LARGEST CIRCULATION OF ANY COMIC MAGAZINE
Captain Marvel
ADVENTURES
No. 21 FEB. 12
A FAWCETT PUBLICATION
10¢
HOLD THAT POSE, ADOLF! THIS ISN'T GOING TO HURT YOU— MUCH!
In this issue... CAPTAIN MARVEL HITS HITLER WITH THE HONESTY RAY

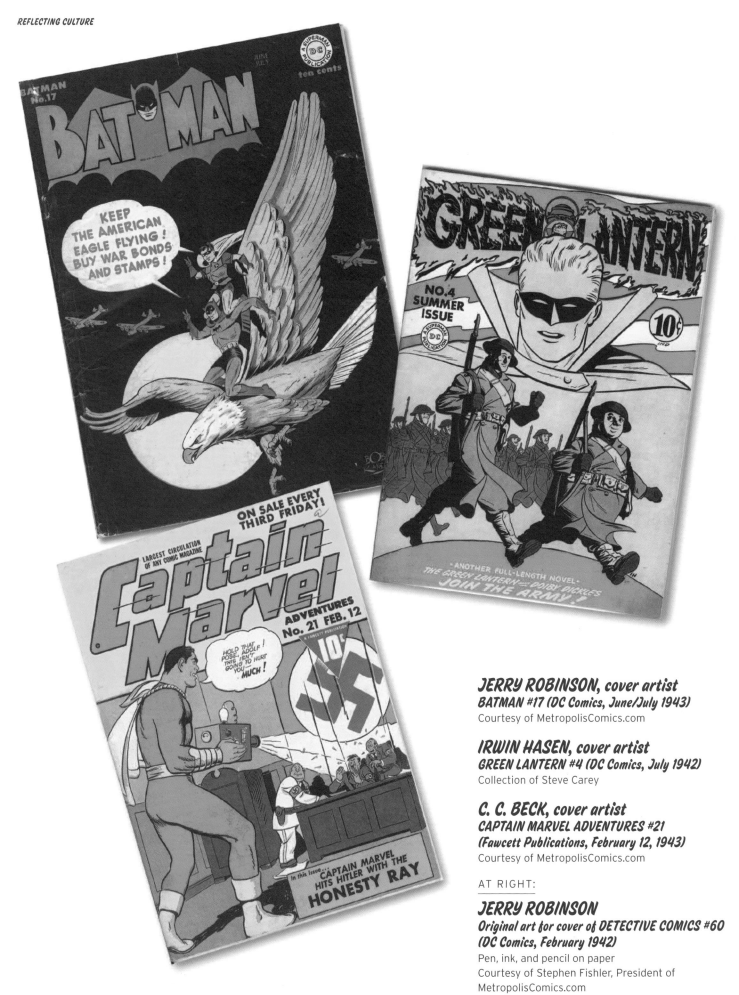

JERRY ROBINSON, cover artist
BATMAN #17 (DC Comics, June/July 1943)
Courtesy of MetropolisComics.com

IRWIN HASEN, cover artist
GREEN LANTERN #4 (DC Comics, July 1942)
Collection of Steve Carey

C. C. BECK, cover artist
CAPTAIN MARVEL ADVENTURES #21
(Fawcett Publications, February 12, 1943)
Courtesy of MetropolisComics.com

AT RIGHT:

JERRY ROBINSON
Original art for cover of DETECTIVE COMICS #60
(DC Comics, February 1942)
Pen, ink, and pencil on paper
Courtesy of Stephen Fishler, President of
MetropolisComics.com

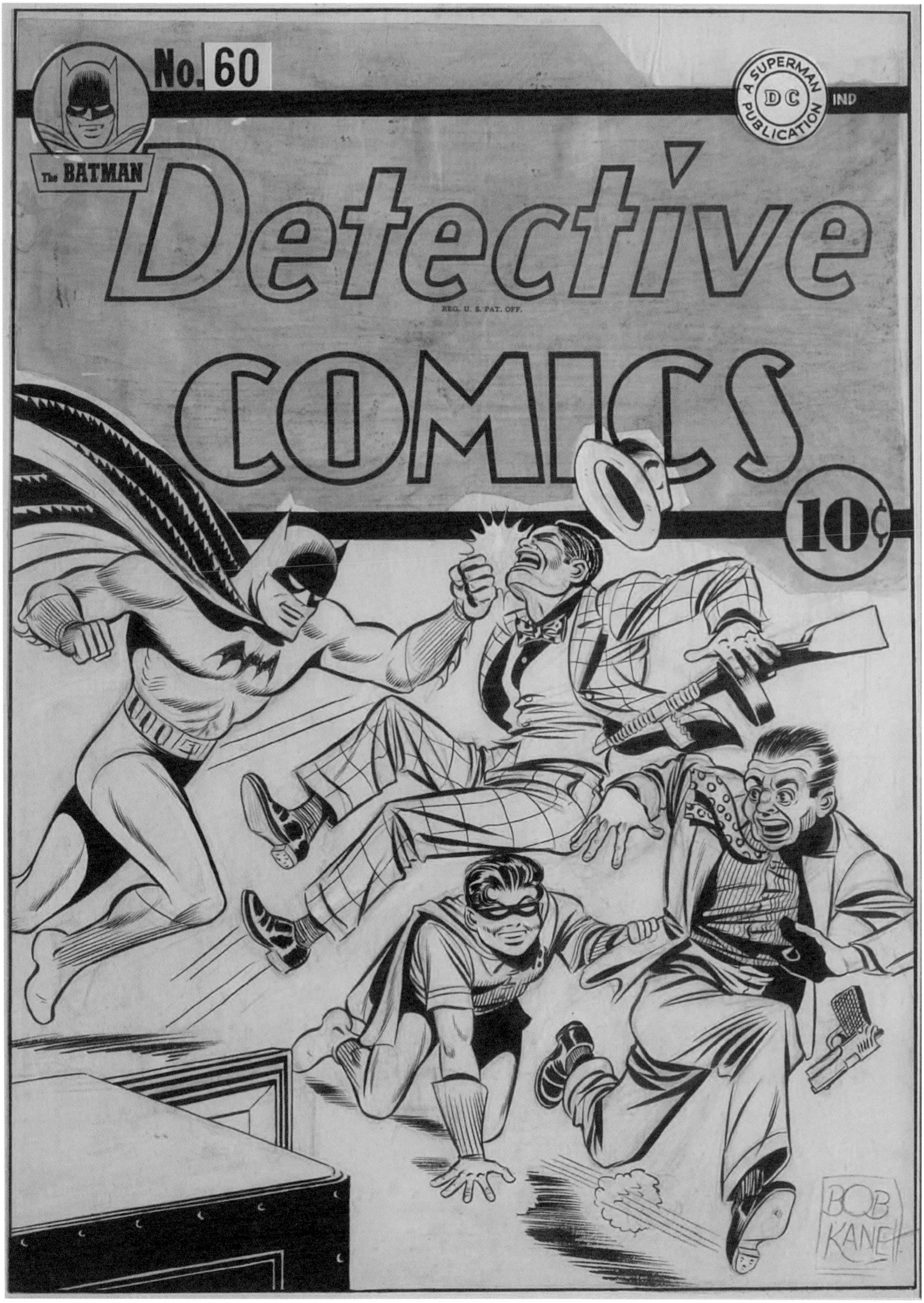
No. 60
The BATMAN
A SUPERMAN DC PUBLICATION
IND
Detective
REG. U. S. PAT. OFF.
COMICS
10¢
BOB KANE

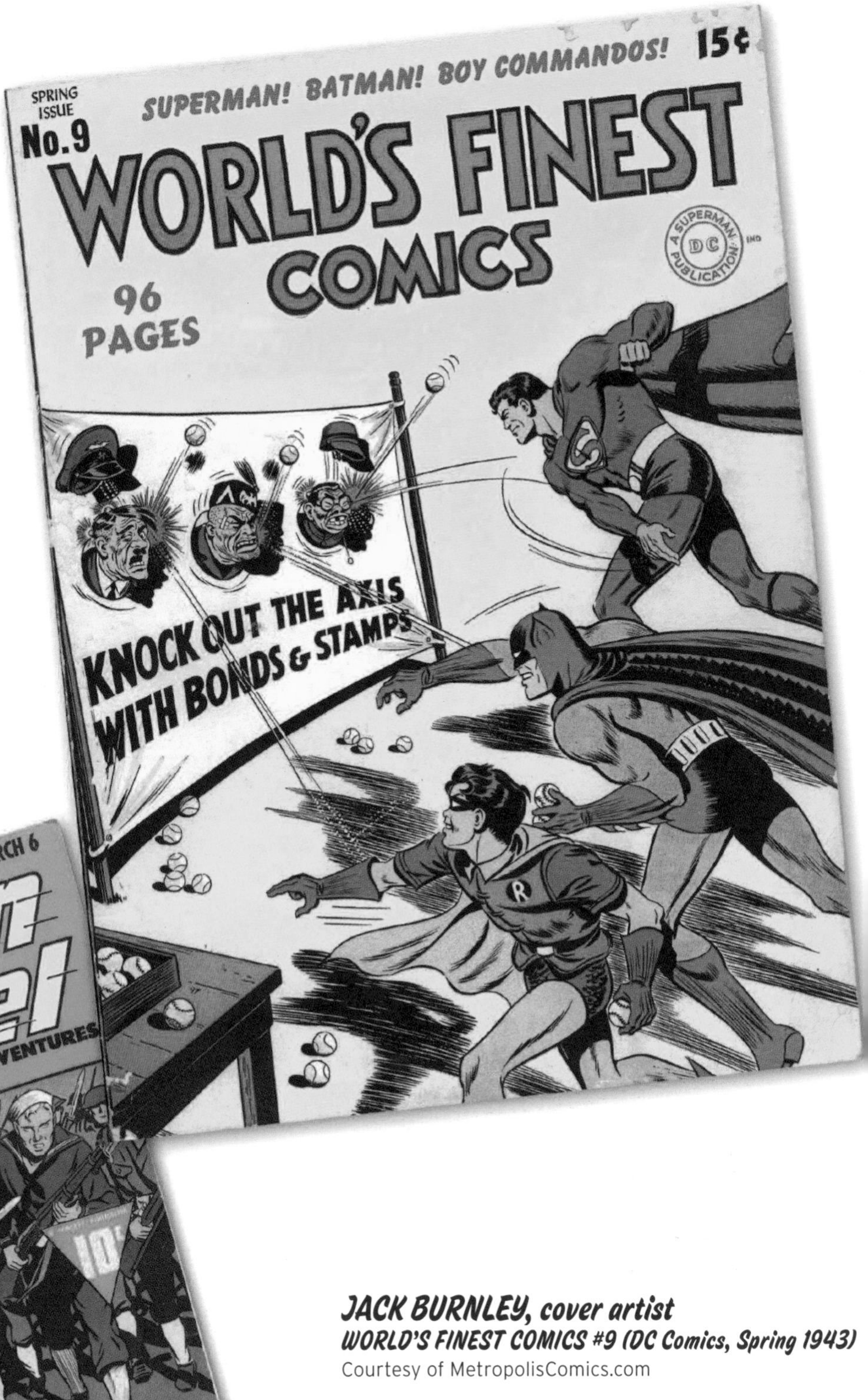
SPRING ISSUE
No.9
SUPERMAN! BATMAN! BOY COMMANDOS!
15¢
WORLD'S FINEST COMICS
A SUPERMAN DC PUBLICATION
96 PAGES
KNOCK OUT THE AXIS WITH BONDS & STAMPS

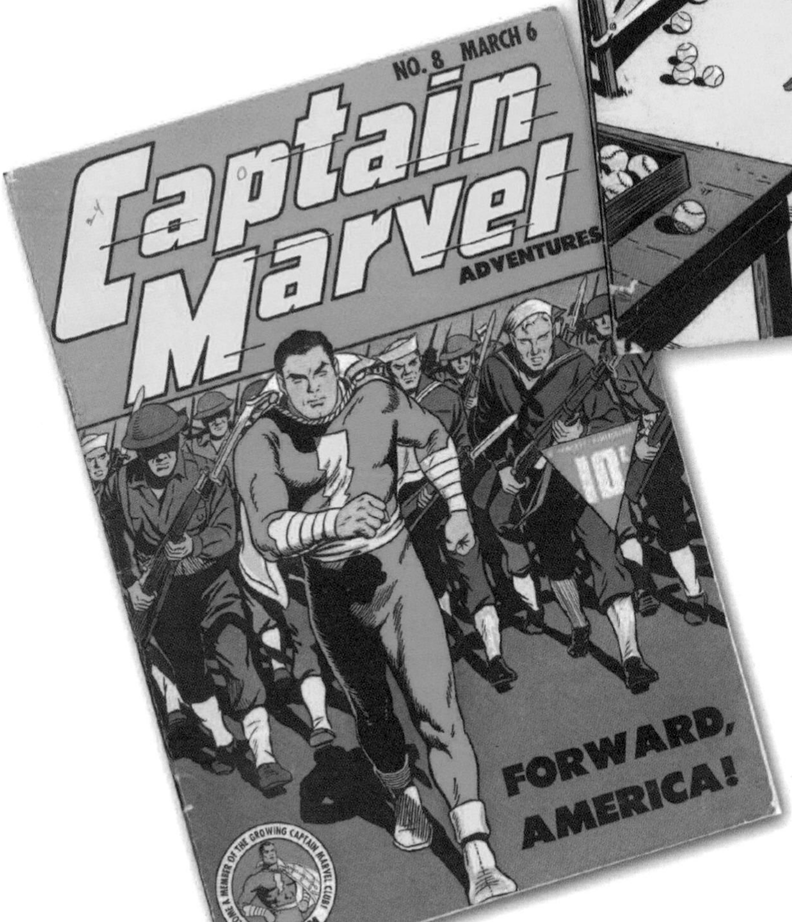
NO. 8 MARCH 6
Captain Marvel
ADVENTURES
10¢
FORWARD, AMERICA!
SHAZAM

JACK BURNLEY, cover artist
WORLD'S FINEST COMICS #9 (DC Comics, Spring 1943)
Courtesy of MetropolisComics.com

C. C. BECK, cover artist
CAPTAIN MARVEL ADVENTURES #8
(Fawcett Publications, March 1942)
Collection of Maggie Thompson

AT RIGHT:

HARRY G. PETER
Original art for WONDER WOMAN unpublished splash page, "Racketeer's Bait!" 1940s
Pen and ink on paper
Courtesy of Stephen Fishler, President of MetropolisComics.com

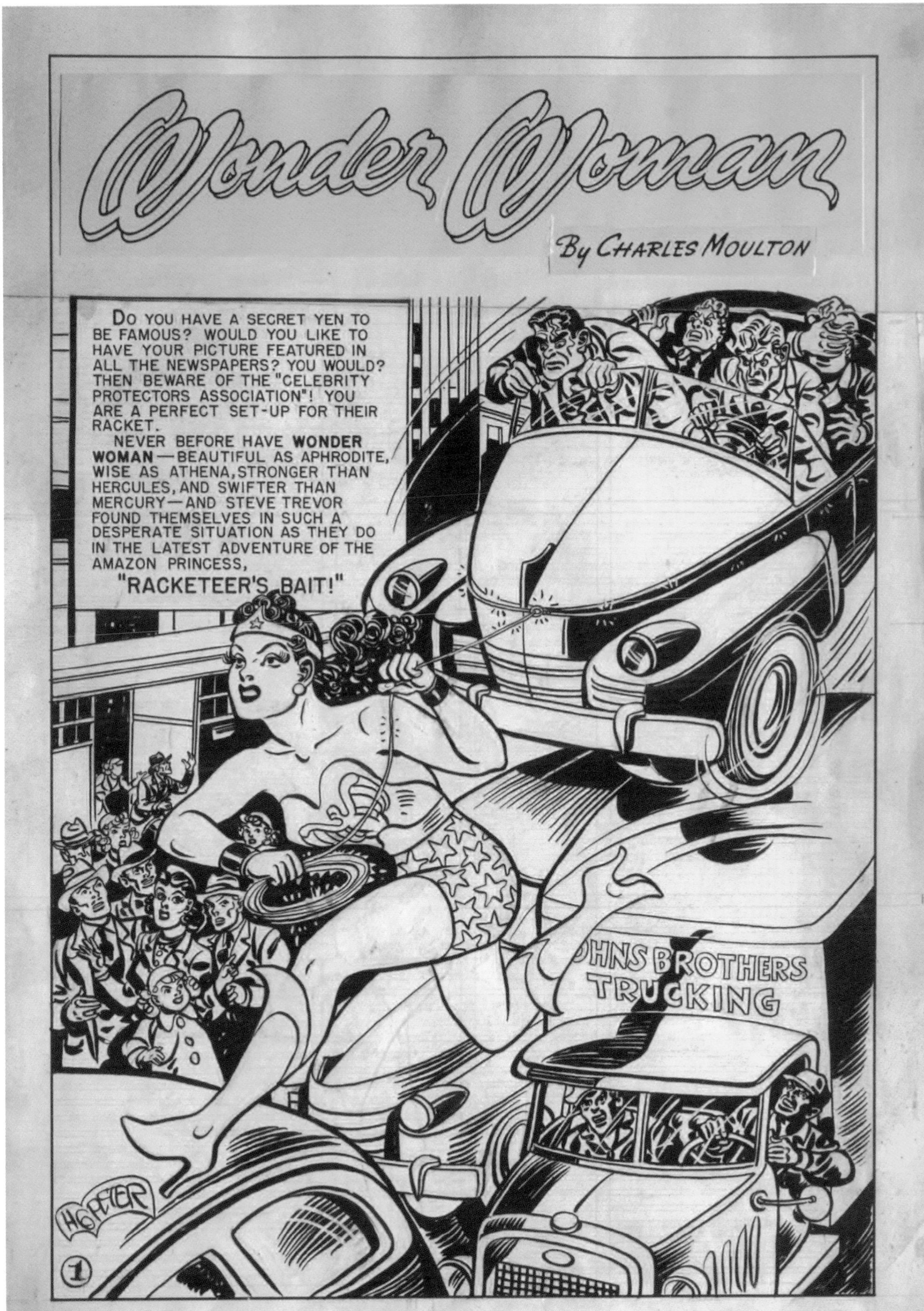
Wonder Woman
By Charles Moulton
DO YOU HAVE A SECRET YEN TO BE FAMOUS? WOULD YOU LIKE TO HAVE YOUR PICTURE FEATURED IN ALL THE NEWSPAPERS? YOU WOULD? THEN BEWARE OF THE "CELEBRITY PROTECTORS ASSOCIATION"! YOU ARE A PERFECT SET-UP FOR THEIR RACKET.
NEVER BEFORE HAVE WONDER WOMAN—BEAUTIFUL AS APHRODITE, WISE AS ATHENA, STRONGER THAN HERCULES, AND SWIFTER THAN MERCURY—AND STEVE TREVOR FOUND THEMSELVES IN SUCH A DESPERATE SITUATION AS THEY DO IN THE LATEST ADVENTURE OF THE AMAZON PRINCESS,
"RACKETEER'S BAIT!"
OHNS BROTHERS TRUCKING
HG PETER
1
WRITTEN OFF 9-30-52

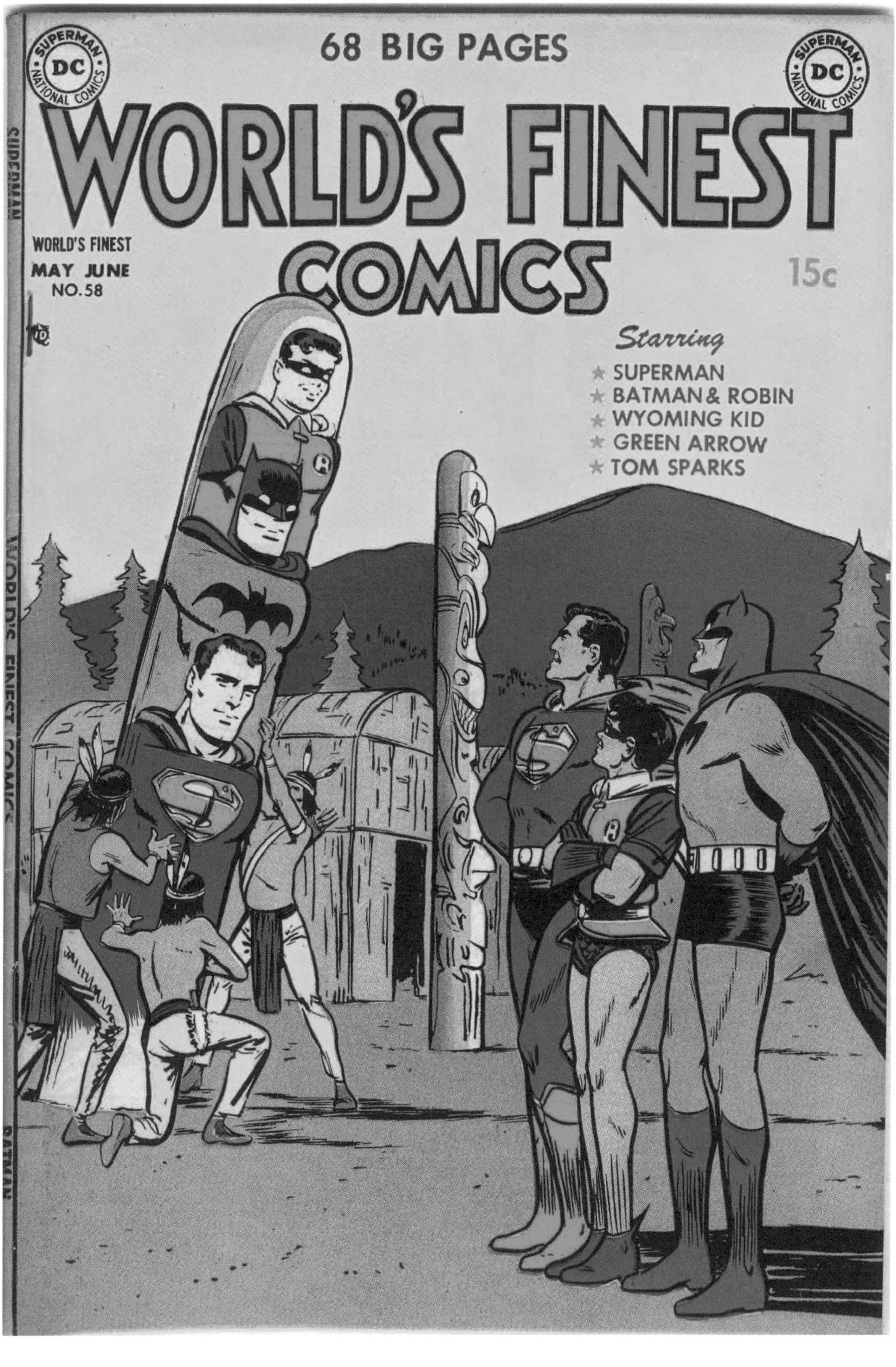
68 BIG PAGES
SUPERMAN DC NATIONAL COMICS
SUPERMAN DC NATIONAL COMICS
WORLD'S FINEST COMICS
WORLD'S FINEST
MAY JUNE
NO.58
15c
Starring
★ SUPERMAN
★ BATMAN & ROBIN
★ WYOMING KID
★ GREEN ARROW
★ TOM SPARKS
SUPERMAN
WORLD'S FINEST COMICS
BATMAN

COLD WAR, CONFORMITY, AND CENSORSHIP:
COMIC BOOK SUPER HEROES IN THE POSTWAR ERA & 1950s

At the end of World War II, super hero comic books suffered a decline in sales when a number of their high-minded, somewhat simplistic characters no longer seemed to address the complexities of the postwar world. DC and other comics increasingly de-emphasized social relevancy in favor of light-hearted juvenile fantasy, reflecting the era's emphasis upon family and social conformity. Although major characters like Superman and Batman continued to sell well, comic book publishers turned to crime, horror, science fiction, westerns, and romance to save the day.

Other comic books revealed serious anxieties about the dawning atomic age and deepening Cold War tensions. As America mobilized for the war against Communism, influences over young people, especially comic books, became hotly contested. Thus, as with rock 'n roll music, the comic book industry found itself increasingly under attack for corrupting impressionable youth and promoting juvenile delinquency. Calls for censorship, comic book burnings, bans, and boycotts culminated in Dr. Frederic Wertham's book, *Seduction of the Innocent* (1954), a lengthy indictment of the comic book industry as subverting America's "adolescent bandits."

To avert the collapse of their business, comic book publishers developed the Comics Code Authority in 1954 to regulate the contents of all comics published with its cover seal of approval—a type of self-censorship by which they gave up much of their creative latitude. Nevertheless, super heroes came back to the forefront and the Silver Age was launched in 1956 with the publication in *Showcase* #4 of a new version of DC's The Flash. Last seen in 1949, the modernized "fastest man alive" evokes Cold War, atom bomb-related anxieties as a police scientist whose immersion in a mysterious combination of chemicals induces his superspeed.

J. WINSLOW MORTIMER, cover artist
WORLD'S FINEST COMICS #58 (DC Comics, May/June 1952)
Collection of Alan Bartholomew

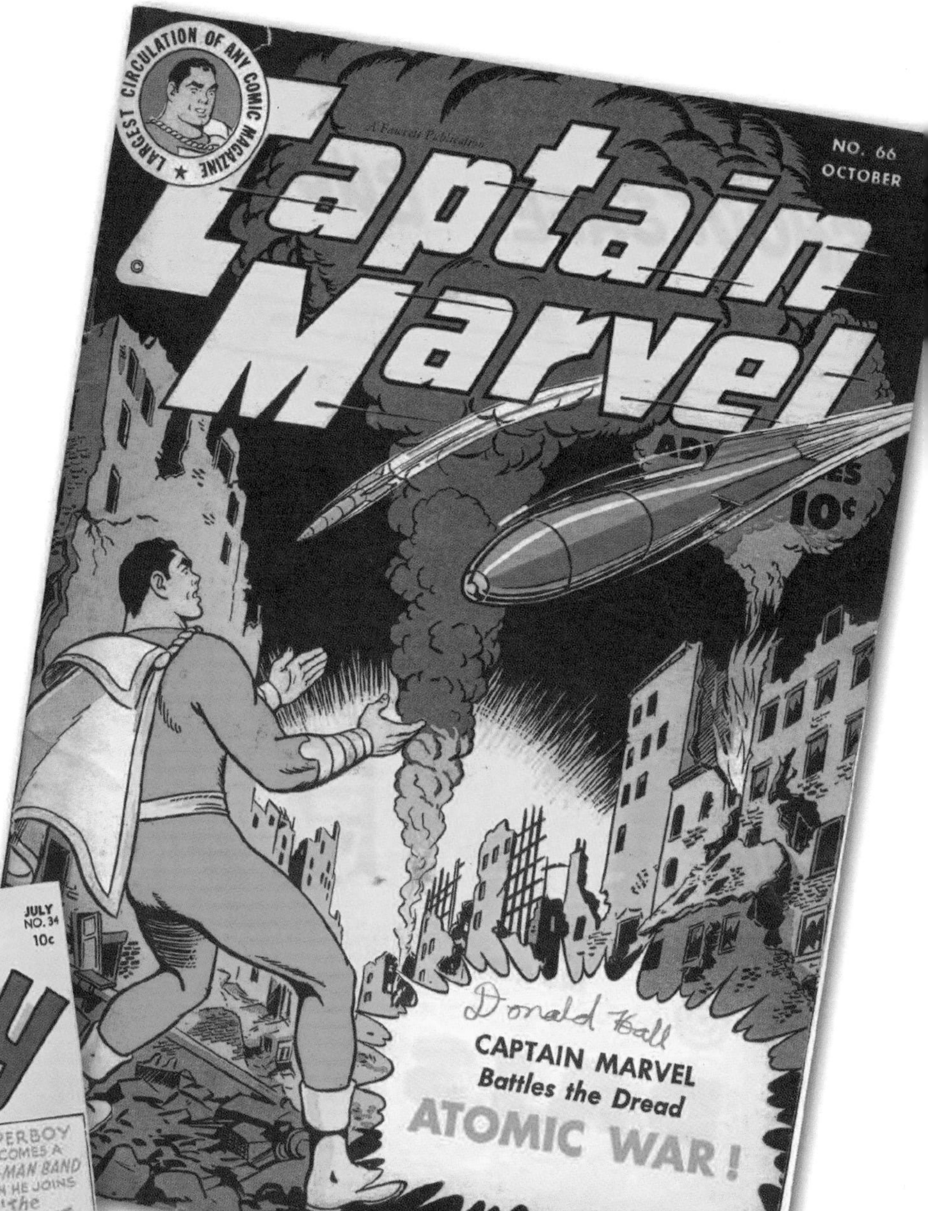
LARGEST CIRCULATION OF ANY COMIC MAGAZINE
Captain Marvel
NO. 66
OCTOBER
10¢
CAPTAIN MARVEL
Battles the Dread
ATOMIC WAR!

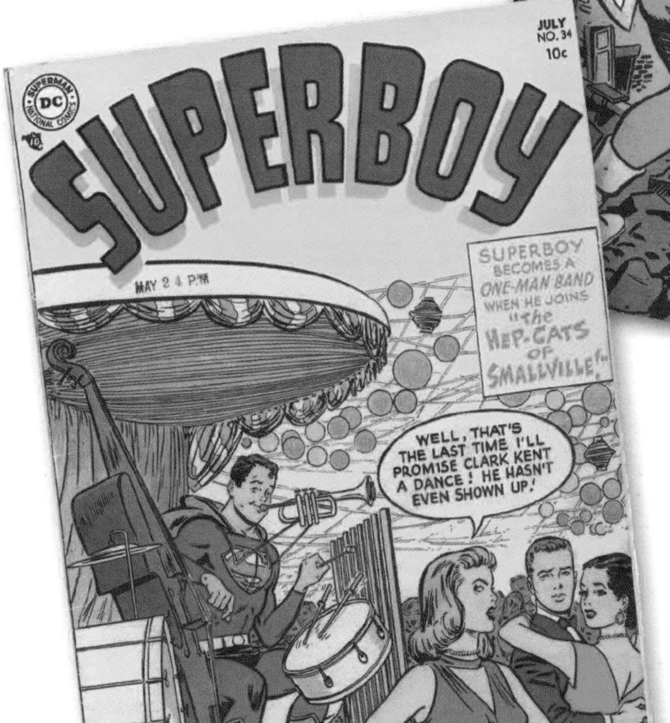
JULY
NO. 34
10¢
SUPERBOY
SUPERBOY BECOMES A ONE-MAN BAND WHEN HE JOINS "the HEP-CATS of SMALLVILLE!"
WELL, THAT'S THE LAST TIME I'LL PROMISE CLARK KENT A DANCE! HE HASN'T EVEN SHOWN UP!

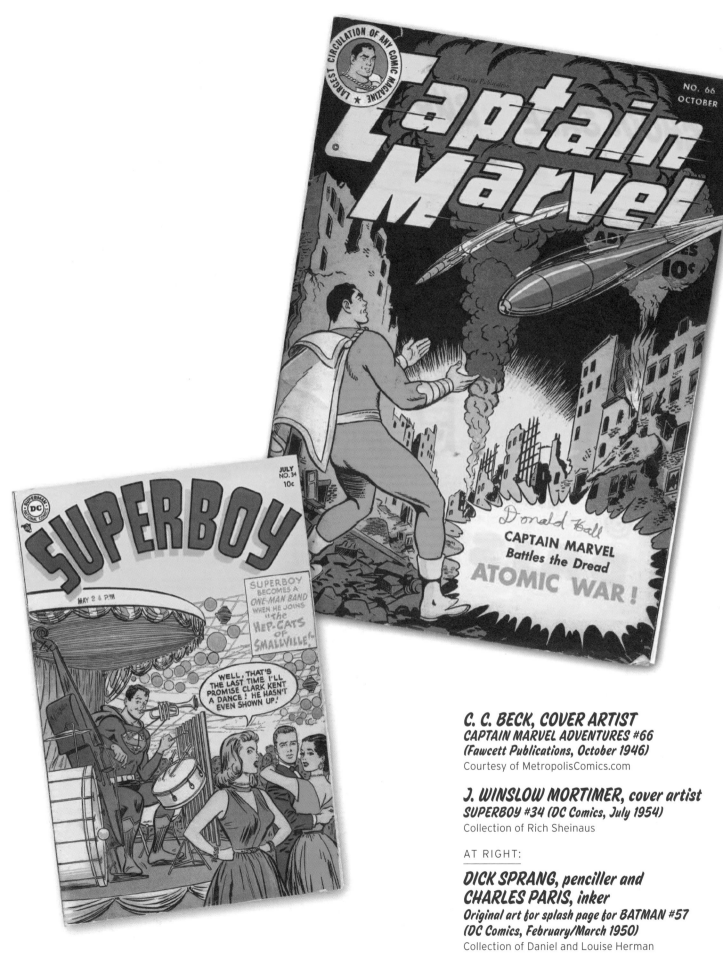

C. C. BECK, COVER ARTIST
CAPTAIN MARVEL ADVENTURES #66
(Fawcett Publications, October 1946)
Courtesy of MetropolisComics.com

J. WINSLOW MORTIMER, cover artist
SUPERBOY #34 (DC Comics, July 1954)
Collection of Rich Sheinaus

AT RIGHT:

DICK SPRANG, penciller and
CHARLES PARIS, inker
Original art for splash page for BATMAN #57
(DC Comics, February/March 1950)
Collection of Daniel and Louise Herman

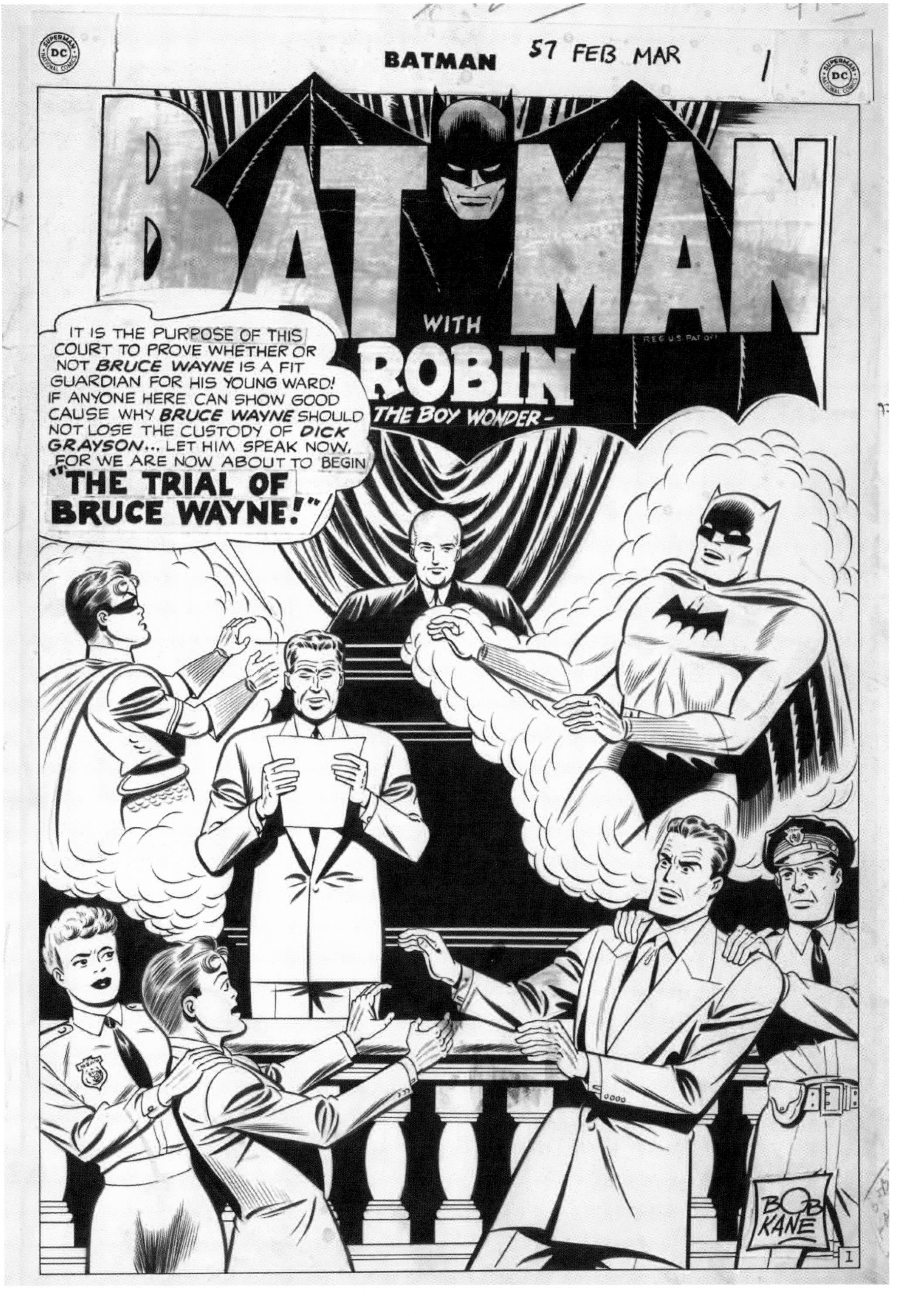

BATMAN 57 FEB MAR 1
BATMAN
WITH ROBIN THE BOY WONDER-
IT IS THE PURPOSE OF THIS COURT TO PROVE WHETHER OR NOT BRUCE WAYNE IS A FIT GUARDIAN FOR HIS YOUNG WARD! IF ANYONE HERE CAN SHOW GOOD CAUSE WHY BRUCE WAYNE SHOULD NOT LOSE THE CUSTODY OF DICK GRAYSON... LET HIM SPEAK NOW, FOR WE ARE NOW ABOUT TO BEGIN "THE TRIAL OF BRUCE WAYNE!"
BOB KANE

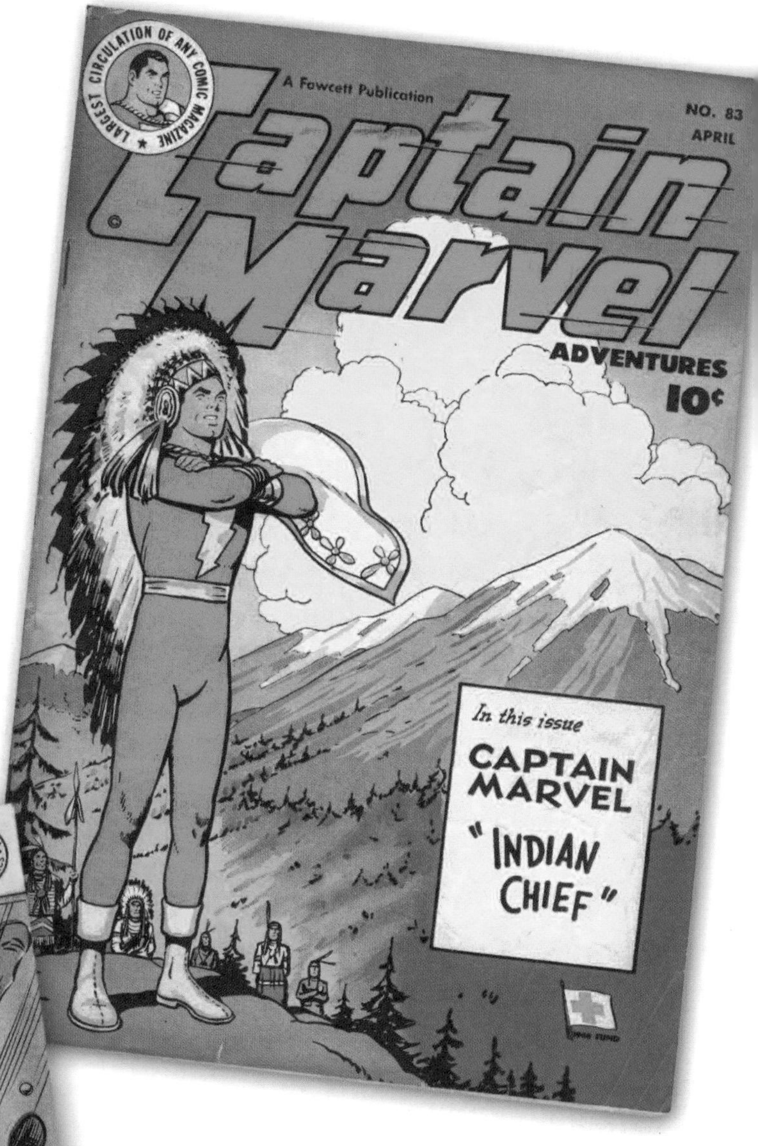
LARGEST CIRCULATION OF ANY COMIC MAGAZINE
A Fawcett Publication
NO. 83
APRIL
Captain Marvel
ADVENTURES
10¢
In this issue
CAPTAIN MARVEL
"INDIAN CHIEF"

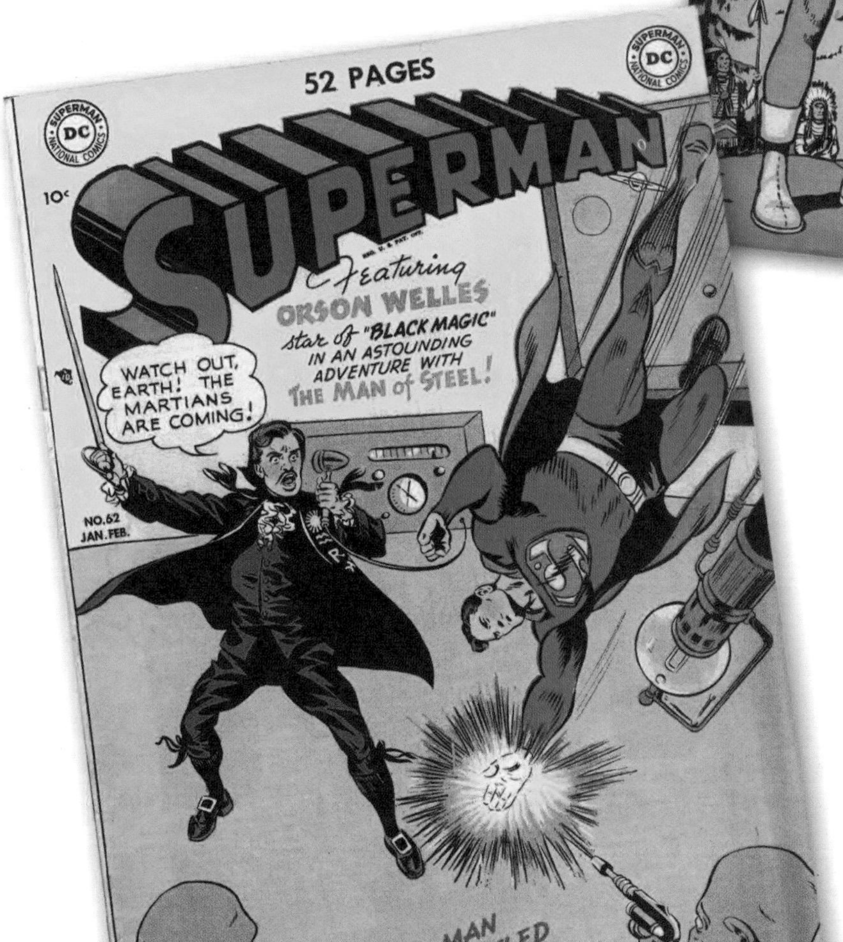
52 PAGES
SUPERMAN
10¢
Featuring
ORSON WELLES
star of "BLACK MAGIC"
IN AN ASTOUNDING ADVENTURE WITH THE MAN of STEEL!
WATCH OUT, EARTH! THE MARTIANS ARE COMING!
NO.62
JAN.FEB.
THE MAN WHO STARTLED AMERICA DOES IT AGAIN!

C. C. BECK, cover artist
CAPTAIN MARVEL ADVENTURES #83
(Fawcett Publications, April 1948)
Collection of Ankur and Indu Jetley

WAYNE BORING, cover penciller and
STAN KAYE, cover inker
SUPERMAN #62 (DC Comics, January/February 1950)
Courtesy of MetropolisComics.com

AT RIGHT:

MARTIN NAYDEL, cover artist
ALL-FLASH #25 (DC Comics, October/November 1946)
Collection of Joseph P. Latino

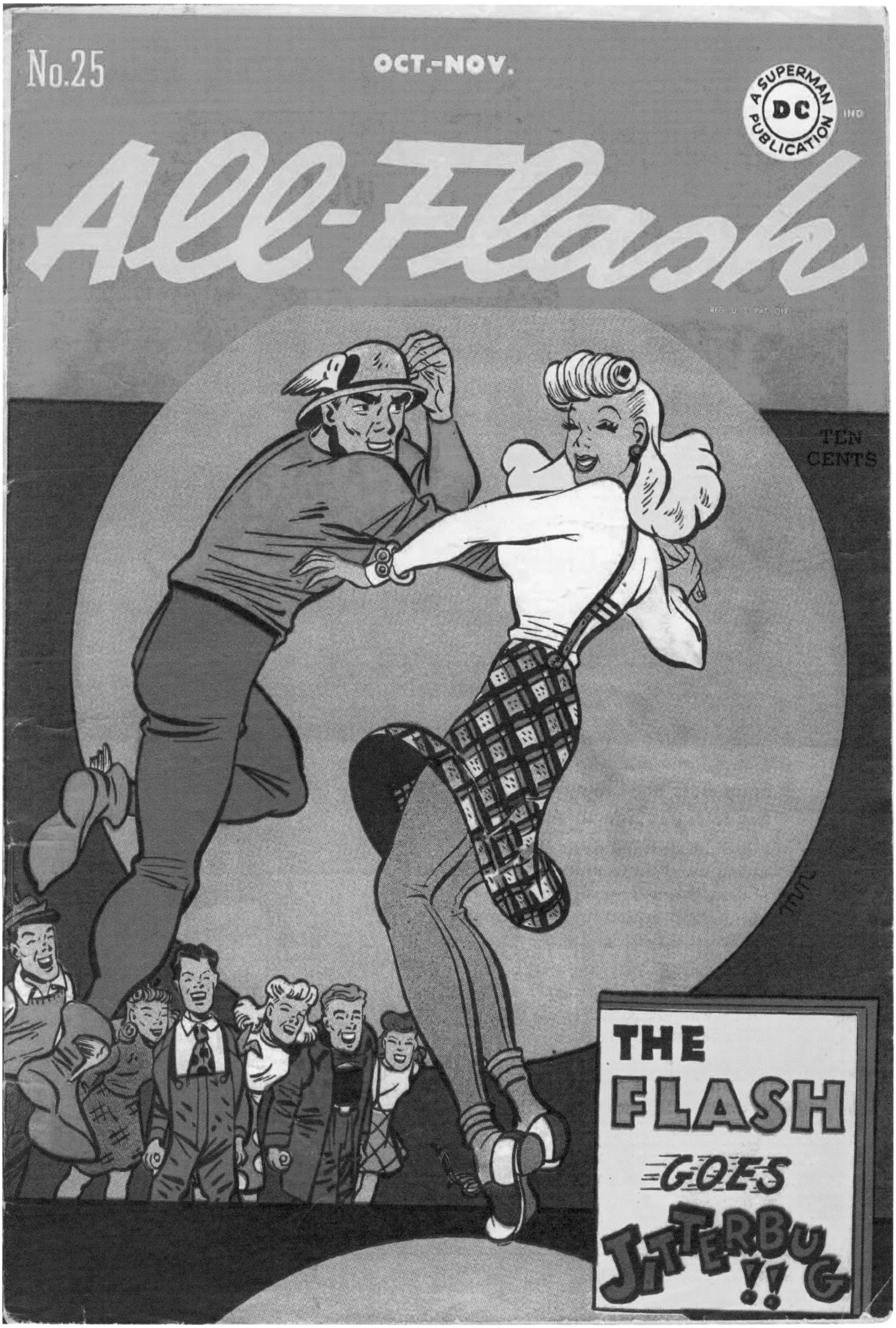
No.25
OCT.-NOV.
A SUPERMAN DC PUBLICATION INC.
All-Flash
TEN CENTS
THE FLASH GOES JITTERBUG!!

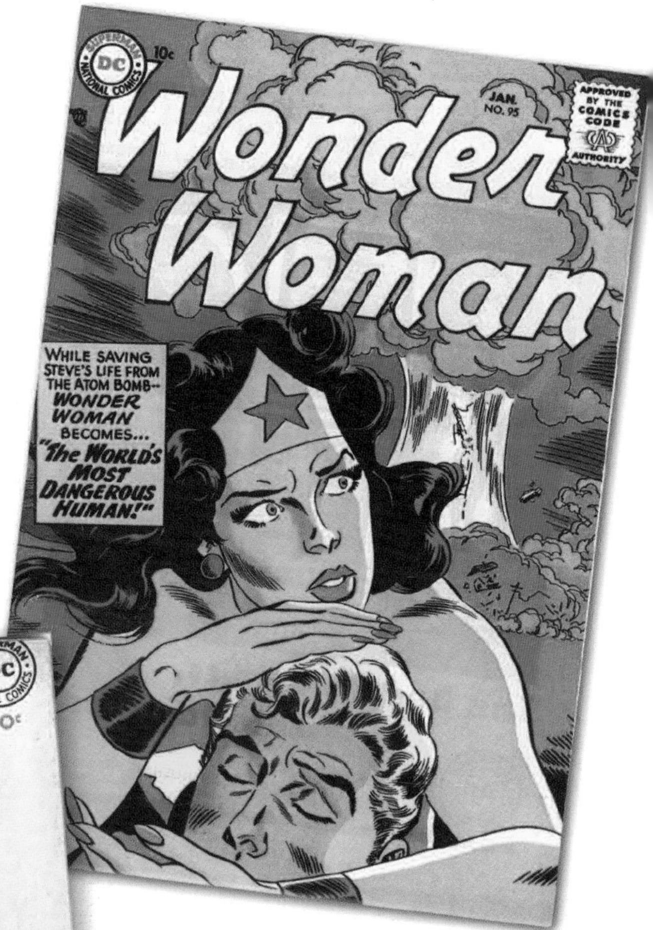
10¢
DC
SUPERMAN NATIONAL COMICS
JAN. NO. 95
APPROVED BY THE COMICS CODE AUTHORITY
Wonder Woman
WHILE SAVING STEVE'S LIFE FROM THE ATOM BOMB-- WONDER WOMAN BECOMES... "The WORLD'S MOST DANGEROUS HUMAN!"

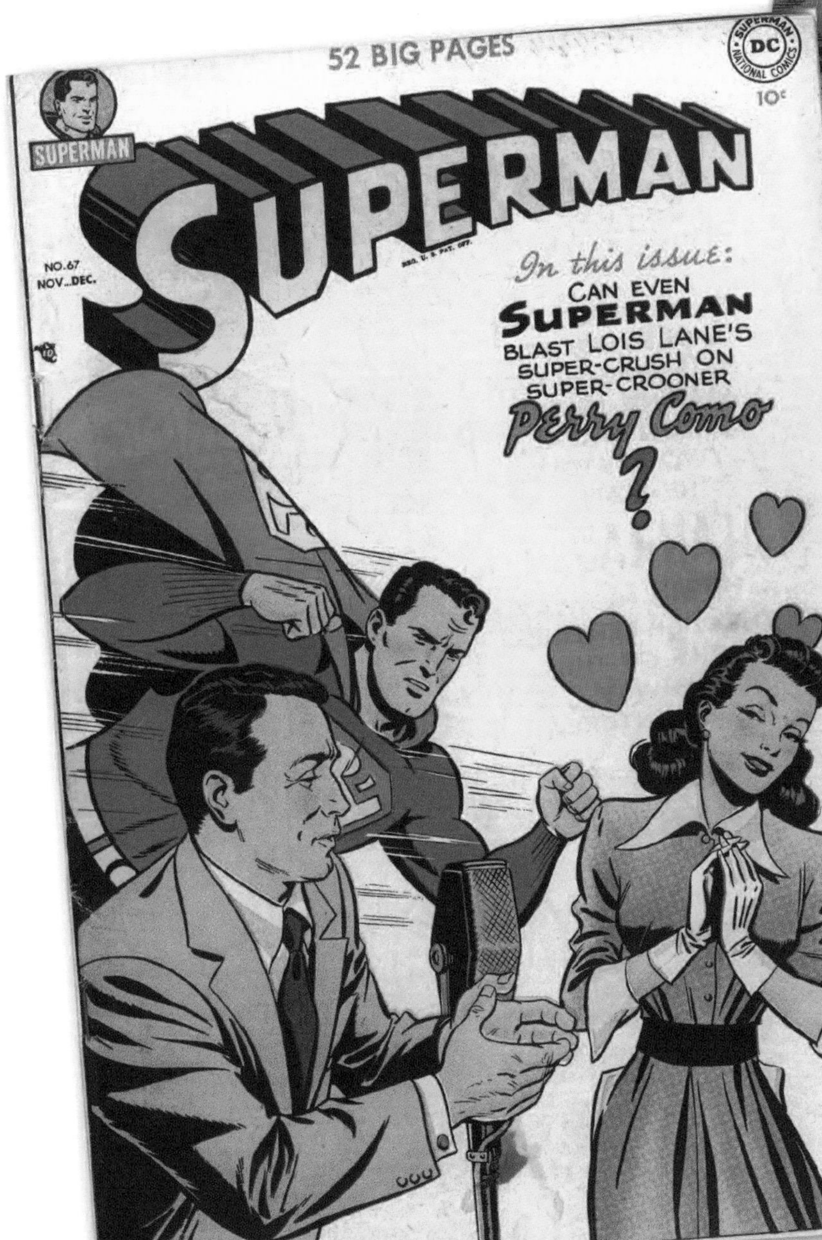
52 BIG PAGES
SUPERMAN
DC
SUPERMAN NATIONAL COMICS
10¢
SUPERMAN
NO. 67
NOV.-DEC.
In this issue:
CAN EVEN SUPERMAN BLAST LOIS LANE'S SUPER-CRUSH ON SUPER-CROONER Perry Como ?

ROSS ANDRU, cover penciller and MIKE ESPOSITO, cover inker
WONDER WOMAN #95
(DC Comics, January 1958)
Collection of Alan Bartholomew

AL PLASTINO, cover penciller and STAN KAYE, cover inker
SUPERMAN #67
(DC Comics, November/December 1950)
Courtesy of MetropolisComics.com

AT RIGHT:

IRWIN HASEN, penciller and BERNARD SACHS, inker
Original art for cover of SENSATION COMICS #96 (DC Comics, March/April 1950)
Pencil and ink on paper
Courtesy of Stephen Fishler,
President of MetropolisComics.com

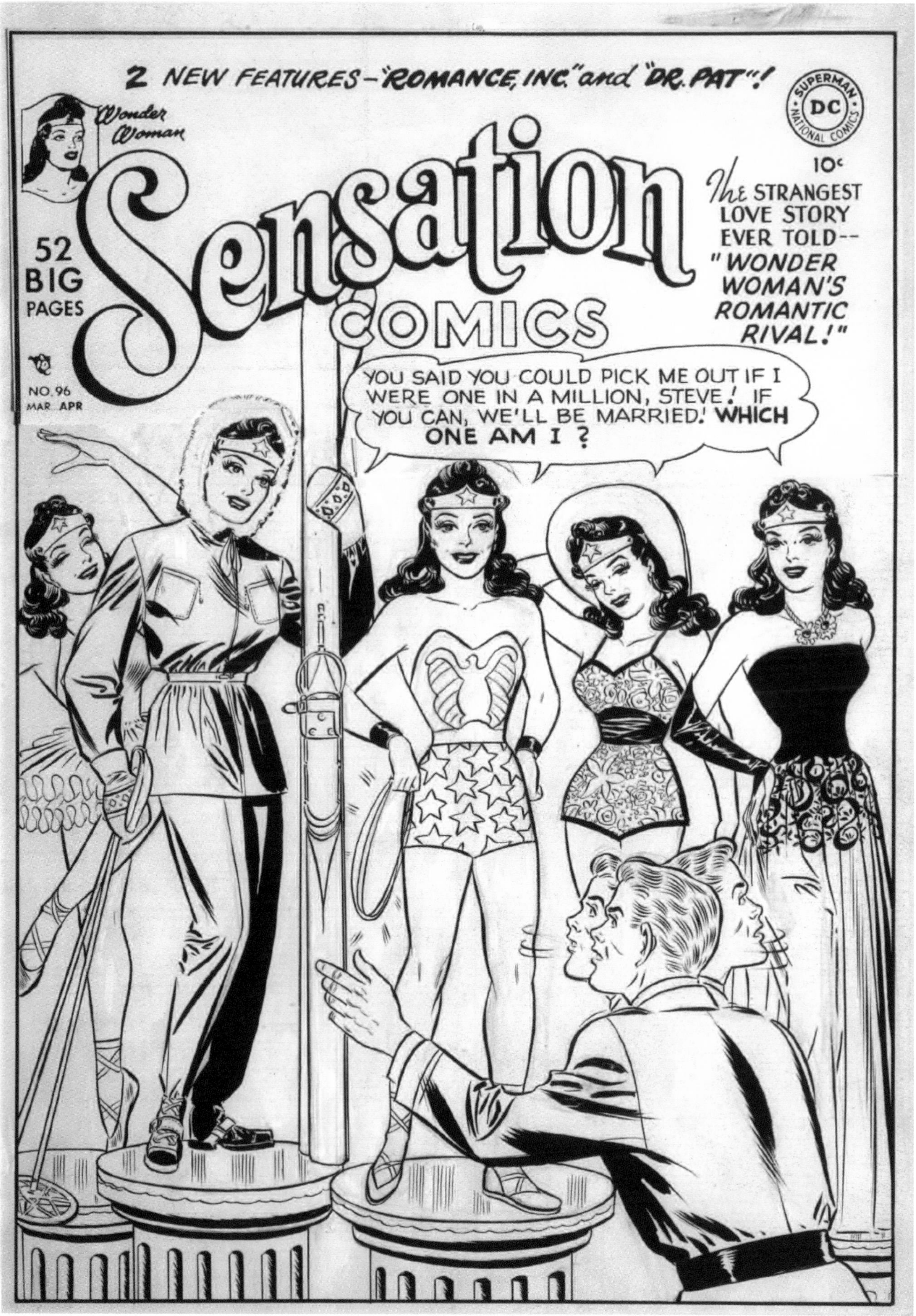
2 NEW FEATURES—"ROMANCE, INC." and "DR. PAT"!
Wonder Woman
SUPERMAN DC NATIONAL COMICS
Sensation COMICS
10¢
52 BIG PAGES
NO. 96 MAR. APR
The STRANGEST LOVE STORY EVER TOLD-- "WONDER WOMAN'S ROMANTIC RIVAL!"
YOU SAID YOU COULD PICK ME OUT IF I WERE ONE IN A MILLION, STEVE! IF YOU CAN, WE'LL BE MARRIED! WHICH ONE AM I ?

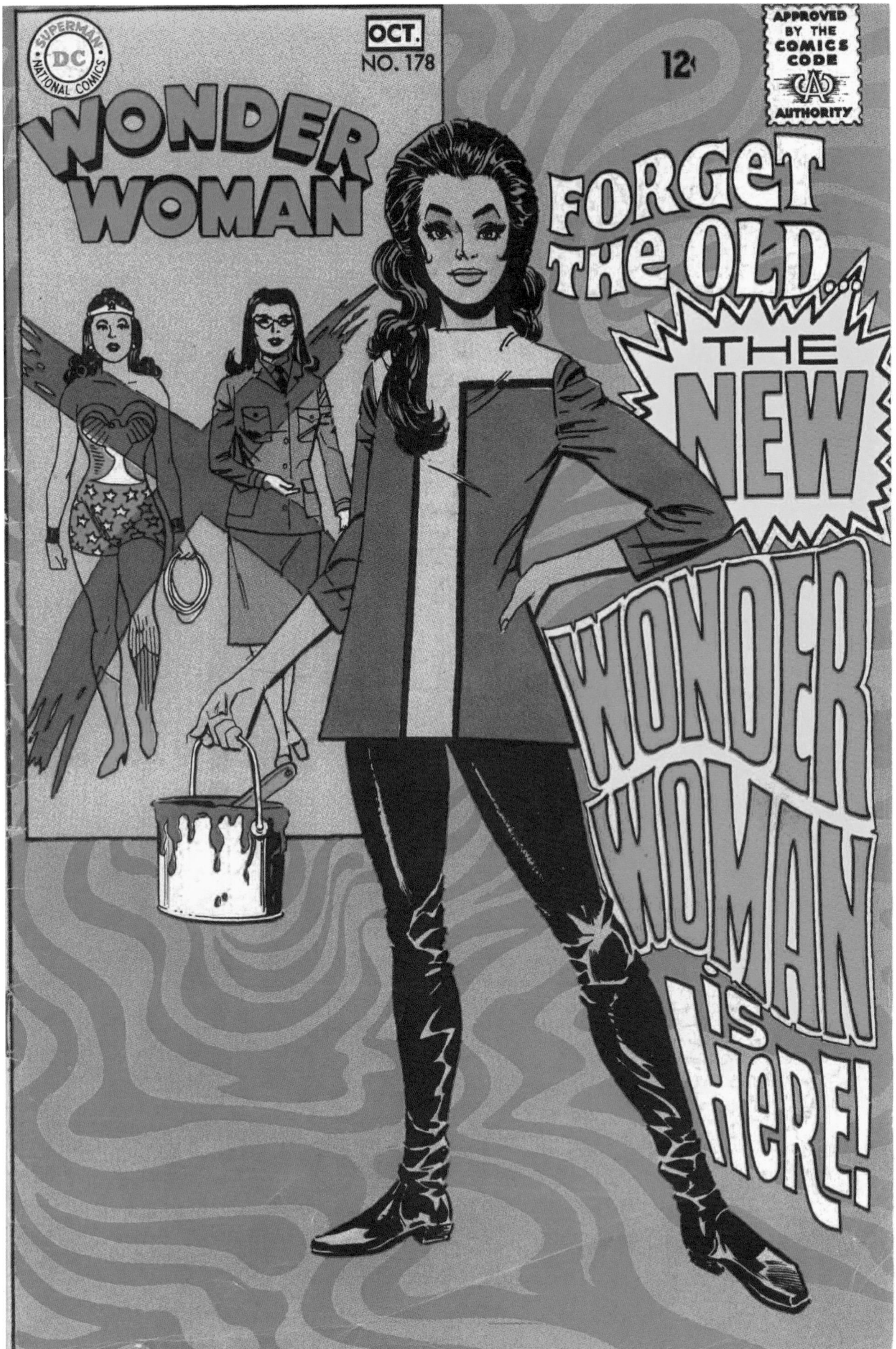
SUPERMAN DC NATIONAL COMICS
OCT.
NO. 178
12¢
APPROVED BY THE COMICS CODE AUTHORITY
WONDER WOMAN
FORGET THE OLD...
THE NEW
WONDER WOMAN
IS HERE!

QUESTIONING AUTHORITY:
COMIC BOOK SUPER HEROES AND SOCIOPOLITICAL CHANGE IN THE 1960s & 70s

Although the DC super hero revival launched the Silver Age (1956-1970), the birth of the "Marvel Age of Comics" with the *Fantastic Four* #1 in November 1961 represented a major shift in the evolution of more human comic book super heroes. In 1962 Spider-Man made his debut as the quintessential Marvel super hero—an adolescent who had to contend with his own foibles, insecurities, and confusion, while "los[ing] out as often as he'd win"—in the words of his co-creator Marvel editor, art director, and chief writer Stan Lee. At a time when youth culture emerged as a major economic, social, and political force, Spider-Man became the most widely imitated archetype in the super hero genre since Superman.

Having successfully tapped into adolescent desires for more believable, morally ambivalent, and complex characters, Marvel generally supplanted DC as the center of the super hero comic book movement at this time. Nevertheless, Neal Adams and Dennis O'Neil's ground-breaking DC series, *Green Lantern/Green Arrow* (1970) immersed its super heroes in the social and political issues of the time: racism, poverty, political corruption, the "generation gap," drug abuse, the plight of Native Americans, pollution, overpopulation, and religious cults.

A greater multicultural diversity in comics also reflected societal concerns, with the introduction of minority characters such as the Black Panther, Luke Cage, Shang Chi, Thunderbird, and others. Introduced in 1963, the culturally diverse, persecuted team of supermutants, the X-Men, has served as a metaphor for prejudice and intolerance. Feminism and women's liberation played a significant role as well, with "Wonder Woman for President" featured on the cover of the first issue of *Ms. Magazine* in 1972.

MIKE SEKOWSKY, *cover penciller and* **DICK GIORDANO,** *cover inker*
WONDER WOMAN #178 (DC Comics, September-October 1968)
Collection of Rich Sheinaus

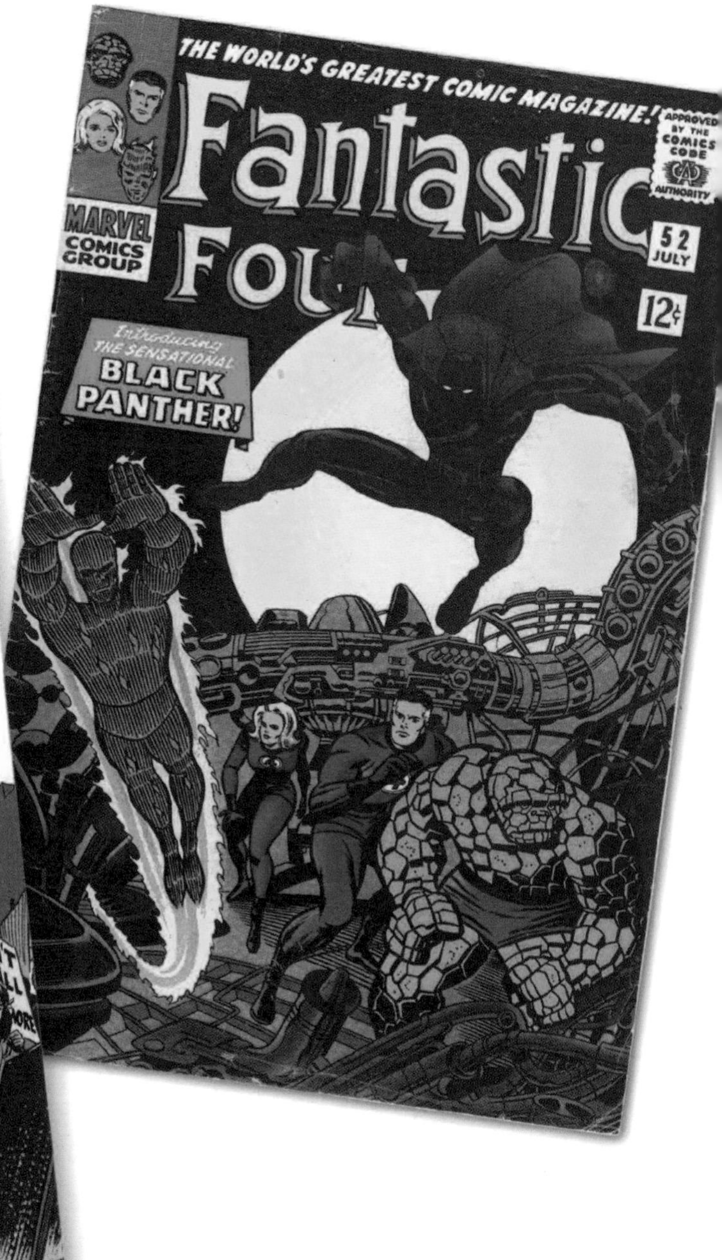
THE WORLD'S GREATEST COMIC MAGAZINE!
APPROVED BY THE COMICS CODE AUTHORITY
Fantastic
FOU
MARVEL COMICS GROUP
52 JULY
12¢
Introducing THE SENSATIONAL
BLACK PANTHER!

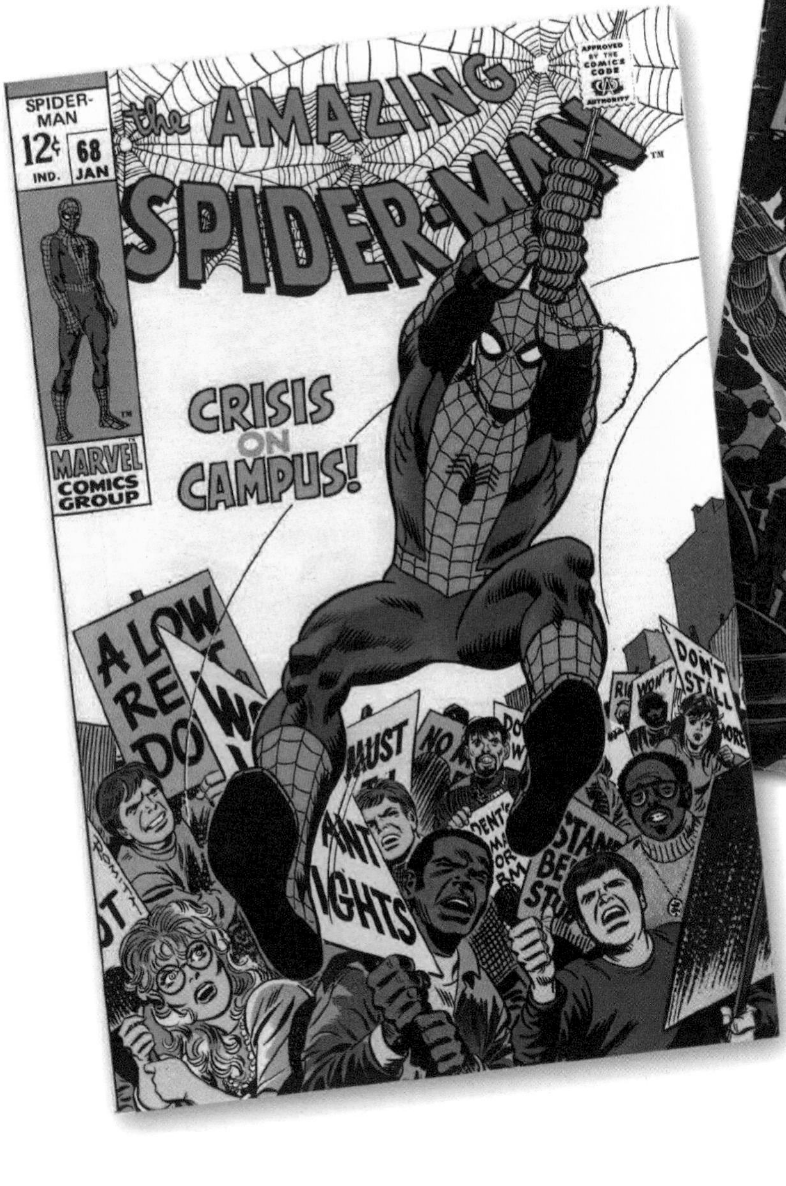
SPIDER-MAN
12¢
68
IND.
JAN
the AMAZING
SPIDER-MAN
APPROVED BY THE COMICS CODE AUTHORITY
MARVEL COMICS GROUP
CRISIS ON CAMPUS!

JOHN ROMITA, SR., cover artist
THE AMAZING SPIDER-MAN #68 (Marvel Comics, January 1969)
Courtesy of MetropolisComics.com

JACK KIRBY, cover penciller and
JOE SINNOTT, cover inker
FANTASTIC FOUR #52 (Marvel Comics, July 1966)
Collection of Michael Uslan

AT RIGHT:

JACK KIRBY, penciller and JOE SINNOTT, inker
Original art for interior page of THE FANTASTIC FOUR #5
(Marvel Comics, July 1962)
Pen and ink on paper
Collection of Joe and Nadia Mannarino

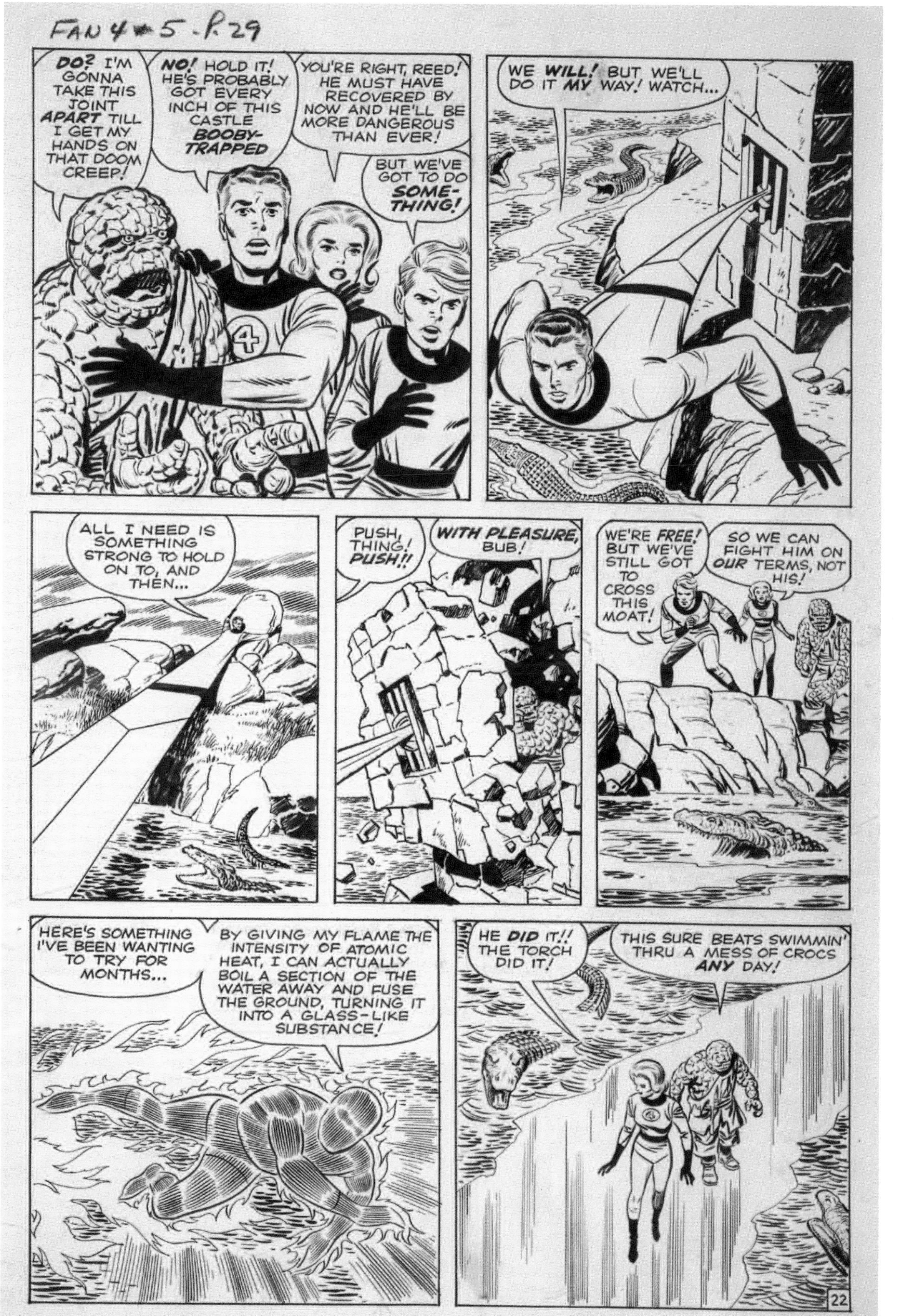
FAN 4 #5 - P. 29
DO? I'M GONNA TAKE THIS JOINT APART TILL I GET MY HANDS ON THAT DOOM CREEP!
NO! HOLD IT! HE'S PROBABLY GOT EVERY INCH OF THIS CASTLE BOOBY-TRAPPED
YOU'RE RIGHT, REED! HE MUST HAVE RECOVERED BY NOW AND HE'LL BE MORE DANGEROUS THAN EVER!
BUT WE'VE GOT TO DO SOME-THING!
WE WILL! BUT WE'LL DO IT MY WAY! WATCH...
ALL I NEED IS SOMETHING STRONG TO HOLD ON TO, AND THEN...
PUSH, THING! PUSH!!
WITH PLEASURE, BUB!
WE'RE FREE! BUT WE'VE STILL GOT TO CROSS THIS MOAT!
SO WE CAN FIGHT HIM ON OUR TERMS, NOT HIS!
HERE'S SOMETHING I'VE BEEN WANTING TO TRY FOR MONTHS...
BY GIVING MY FLAME THE INTENSITY OF ATOMIC HEAT, I CAN ACTUALLY BOIL A SECTION OF THE WATER AWAY AND FUSE THE GROUND, TURNING IT INTO A GLASS-LIKE SUBSTANCE!
HE DID IT!! THE TORCH DID IT!
THIS SURE BEATS SWIMMIN' THRU A MESS OF CROCS ANY DAY!
22
29.

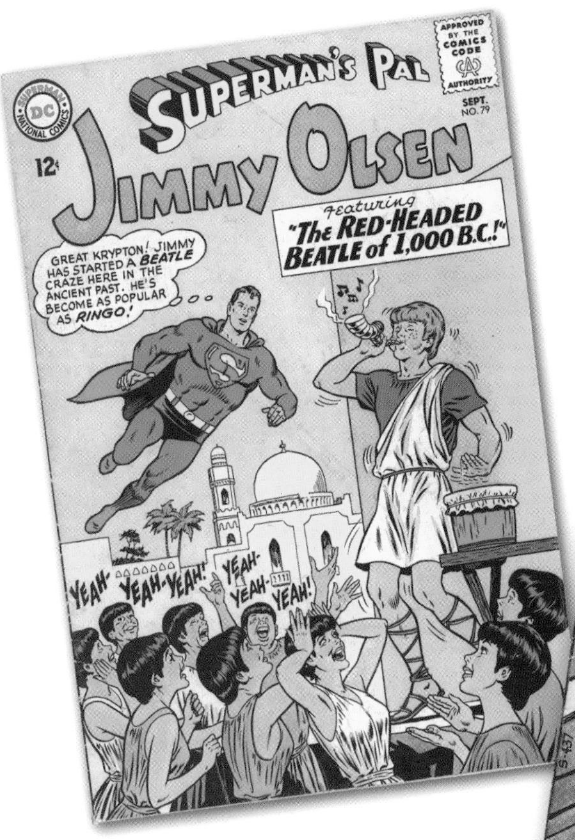
SUPERMAN NATIONAL COMICS DC
APPROVED BY THE COMICS CODE AUTHORITY
SUPERMAN'S PAL
JIMMY OLSEN
12¢
SEPT. NO. 79
featuring "The RED-HEADED BEATLE of 1,000 B.C.!"
GREAT KRYPTON! JIMMY HAS STARTED A BEATLE CRAZE HERE IN THE ANCIENT PAST. HE'S BECOME AS POPULAR AS RINGO!
YEAH-YEAH-YEAH! YEAH-YEAH-YEAH!

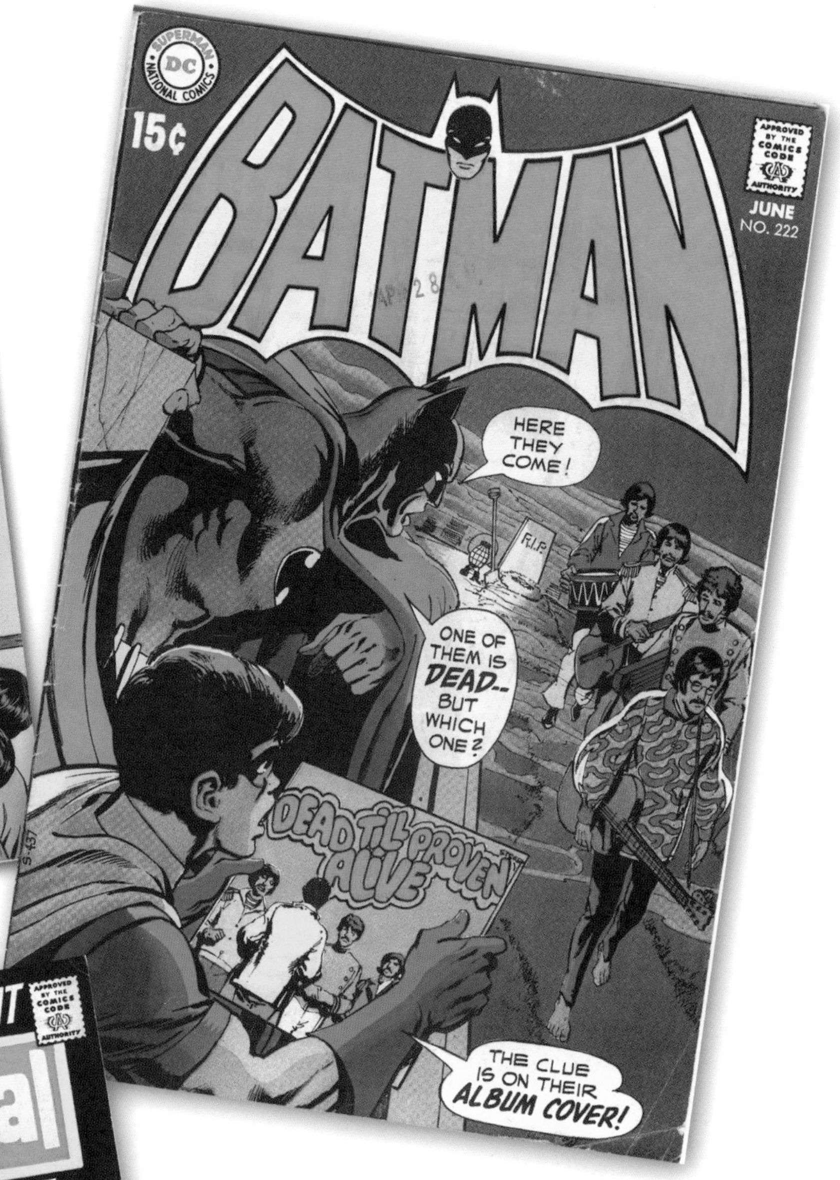
SUPERMAN NATIONAL COMICS DC
15¢
BATMAN
APPROVED BY THE COMICS CODE AUTHORITY
JUNE NO. 222
HERE THEY COME!
ONE OF THEM IS DEAD-- BUT WHICH ONE?
DEAD TIL PROVEN ALIVE
THE CLUE IS ON THEIR ALBUM COVER!

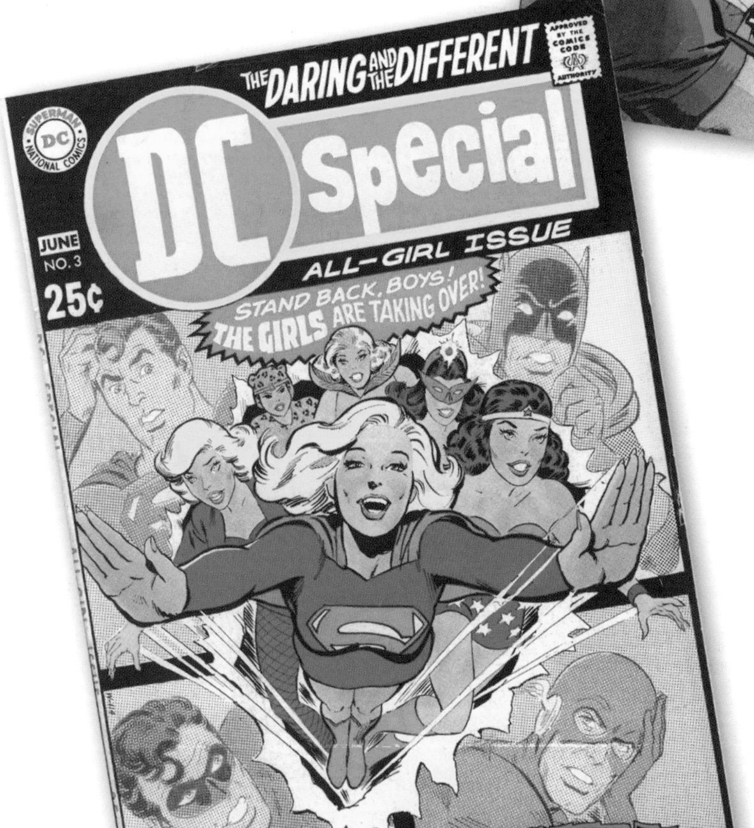
THE DARING AND THE DIFFERENT
APPROVED BY THE COMICS CODE AUTHORITY
SUPERMAN NATIONAL COMICS DC
DC Special
JUNE NO. 3
25¢
ALL-GIRL ISSUE
STAND BACK, BOYS! THE GIRLS ARE TAKING OVER!
SEE OUR FIGHTING FEMALES DO THEIR THING

***CURT SWAN*, cover penciller and**
***GEORGE KLEIN*, cover inker**
SUPERMAN'S PAL JIMMY OLSEN #79
(DC Comics, September 1964)
Collection of Michael Uslan

***NEAL ADAMS*, cover penciller and**
***DICK GIORDANO*, cover inker**
BATMAN #222 (DC Comics, June 1970)
Collection of Rich Sheinaus

***NEAL ADAMS*, cover penciller and**
***NICK CARDY*, cover inker**
DC SPECIAL NO. 3 All-Girl Issue
(DC Comics, April/June 1969)
Courtesy of MetropolisComics.com

AT RIGHT:

JOHN ROMITA, SR.
Original art for the cover of THE AMAZING SPIDER-MAN #75 (Marvel Comics, August 1969)
Pen and ink on paper
Collection of Srihari S. Naidu, M.D.

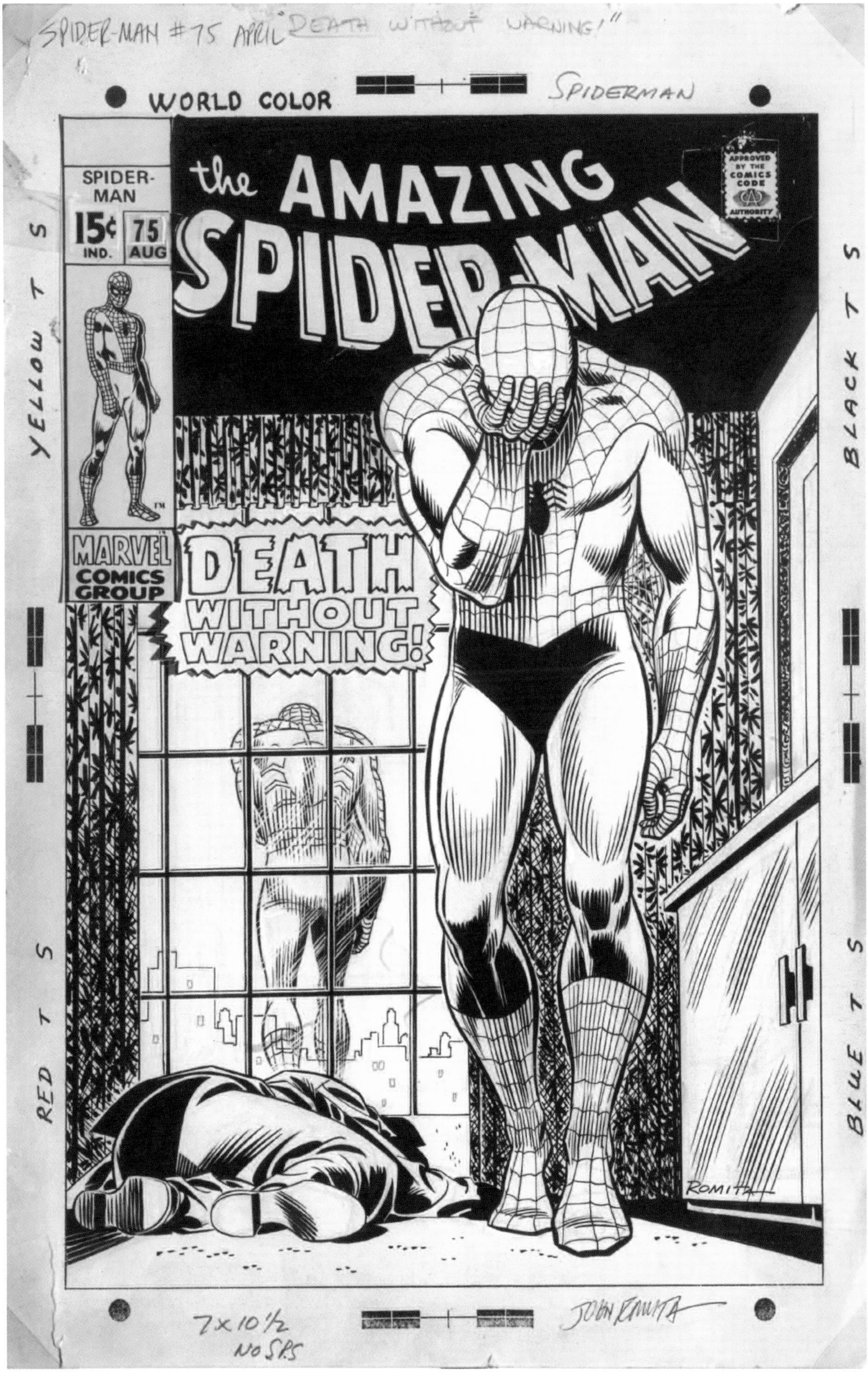
SPIDER-MAN #75 APRIL "DEATH WITHOUT WARNING!"
WORLD COLOR
SPIDERMAN
SPIDER-MAN
15¢ IND.
75 AUG
the AMAZING SPIDER-MAN
APPROVED BY THE COMICS CODE AUTHORITY
MARVEL COMICS GROUP
DEATH WITHOUT WARNING!
YELLOW T S
RED T S
BLACK T S
BLUE T S
ROMITA
JOHN ROMITA
7x10½
NO S.P.S

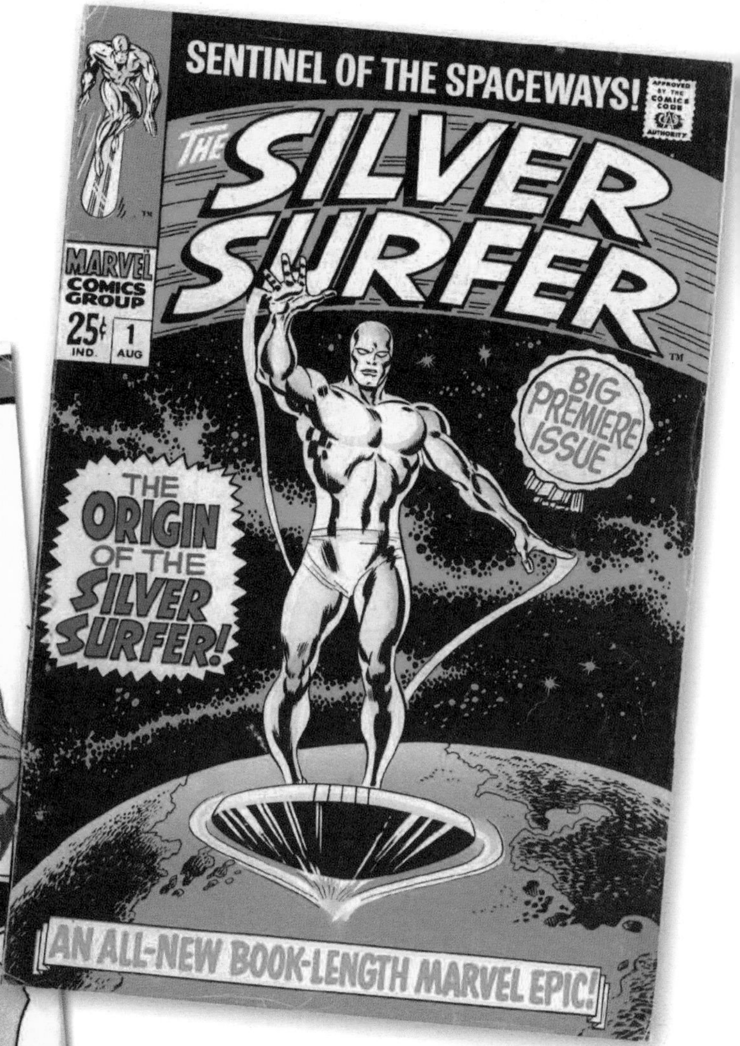
SENTINEL OF THE SPACEWAYS!
THE SILVER SURFER
MARVEL COMICS GROUP
25¢ IND.
1 AUG
BIG PREMIERE ISSUE
THE ORIGIN OF THE SILVER SURFER!
AN ALL-NEW BOOK-LENGTH MARVEL EPIC!

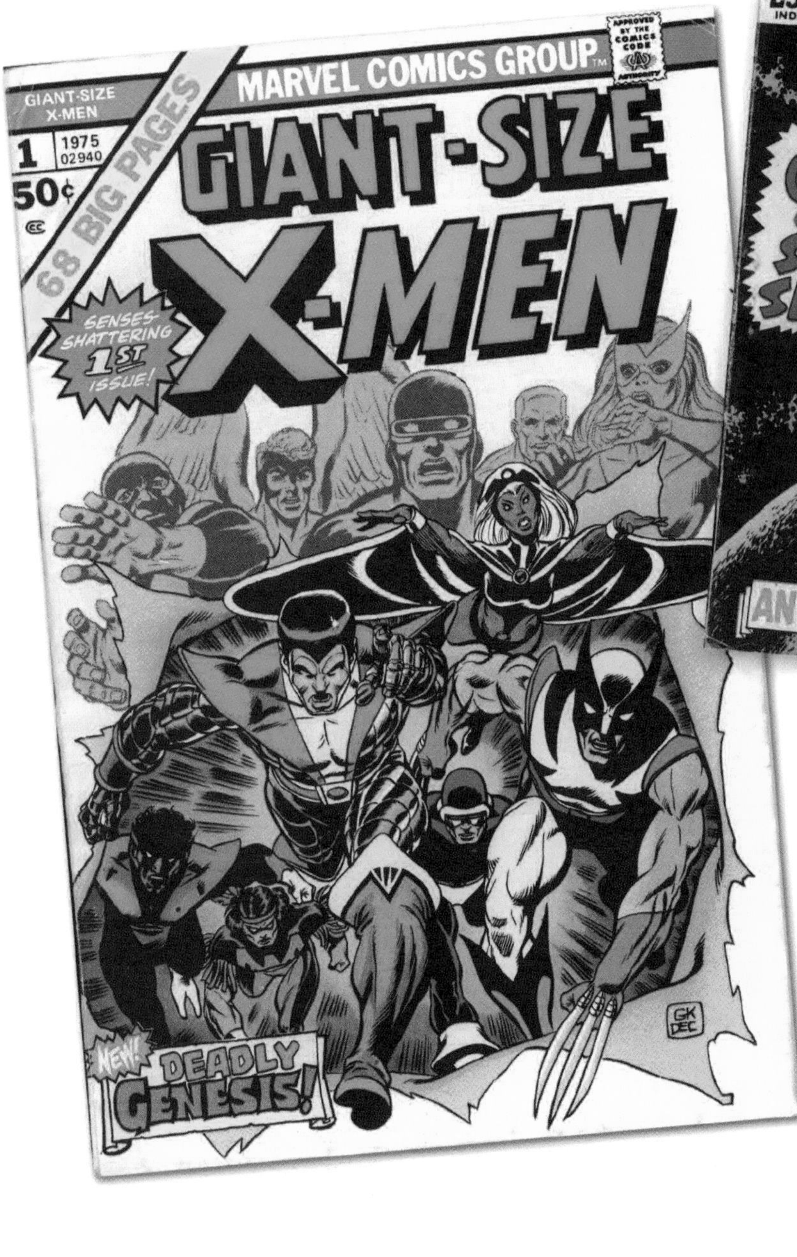
MARVEL COMICS GROUP
GIANT-SIZE X-MEN
1 1975 02940
50¢
68 BIG PAGES
GIANT-SIZE
X-MEN
SENSES-SHATTERING 1ST ISSUE!
NEW! DEADLY GENESIS!
GK DEC

JOHN BUSCEMA, cover penciller and
JOE SINNOTT, cover inker
THE SILVER SURFER #1 (Marvel Comics, August 1968)
Collection of Michael Uslan

DAVE COCKRUM, cover artist
GIANT SIZE X-MEN #1 (Marvel Comics, Summer 1975)
Collection of Michael Uslan

AT RIGHT:

CARMINE INFANTINO, penciller and
MURPHY ANDERSON, inker
Original art for cover of JUSTICE LEAGUE OF AMERICA #57
(DC Comics, November 1967)
Pen and ink on paper
Courtesy of Stephen Fishler, President of MetropolisComics.com

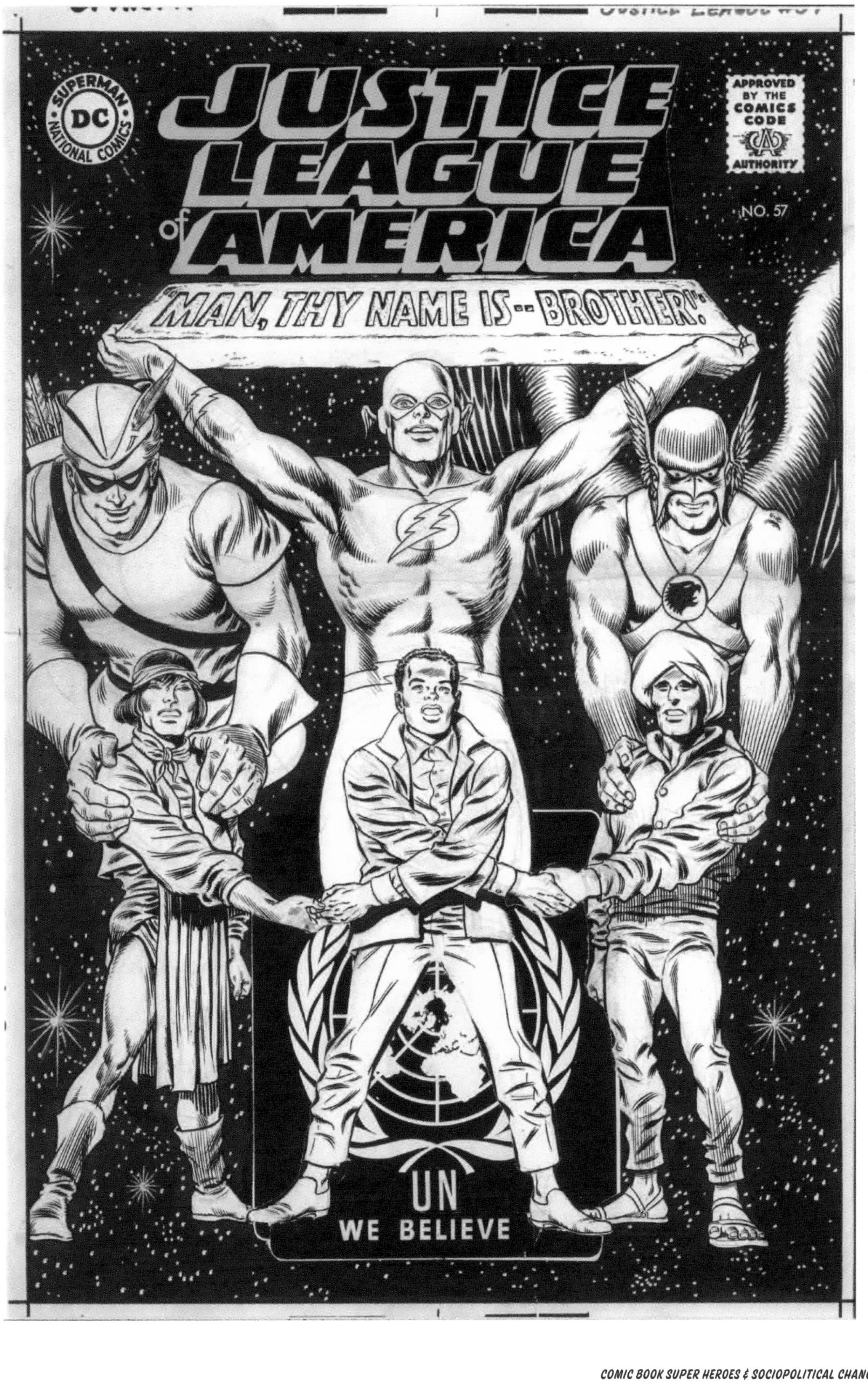
JUSTICE LEAGUE of AMERICA
SUPERMAN DC NATIONAL COMICS
APPROVED BY THE COMICS CODE AUTHORITY
NO. 57
"MAN, THY NAME IS--BROTHER!"
UN
WE BELIEVE

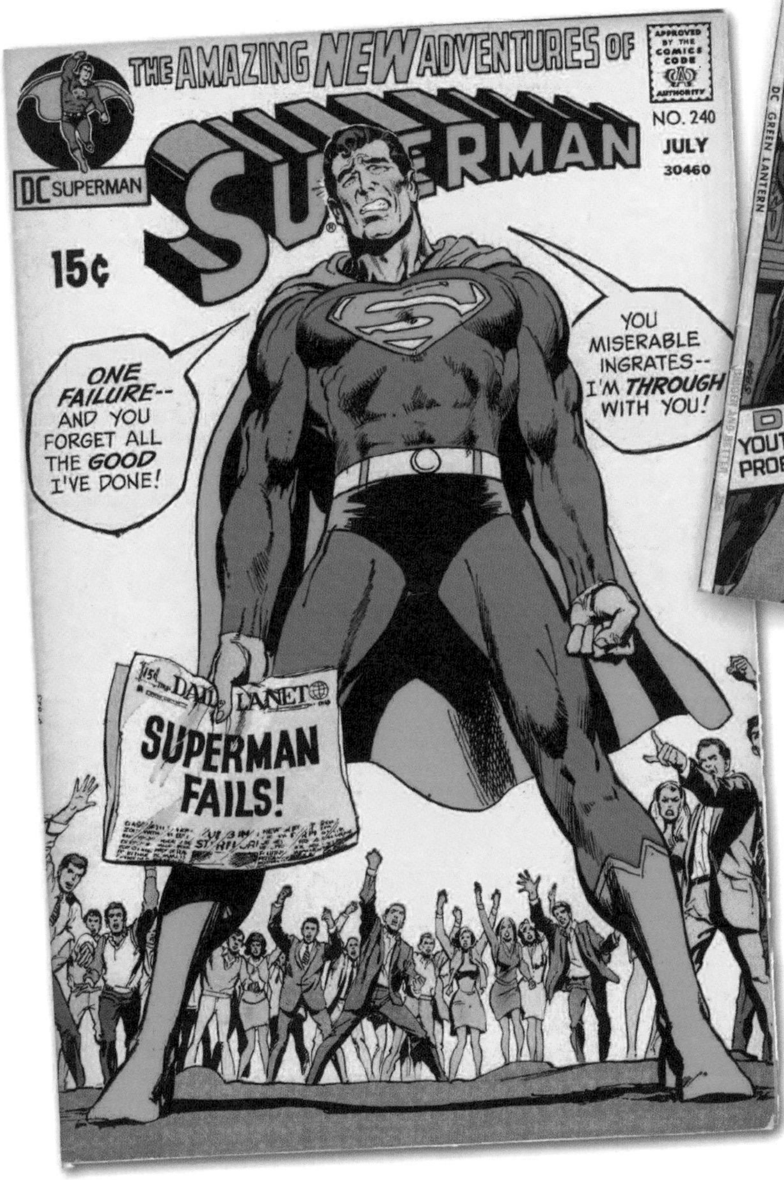
THE AMAZING NEW ADVENTURES OF
SUPERMAN
APPROVED BY THE COMICS CODE AUTHORITY
NO. 240
JULY
30460
DC SUPERMAN
15¢
ONE FAILURE-- AND YOU FORGET ALL THE GOOD I'VE DONE!
YOU MISERABLE INGRATES-- I'M THROUGH WITH YOU!
SUPERMAN FAILS!

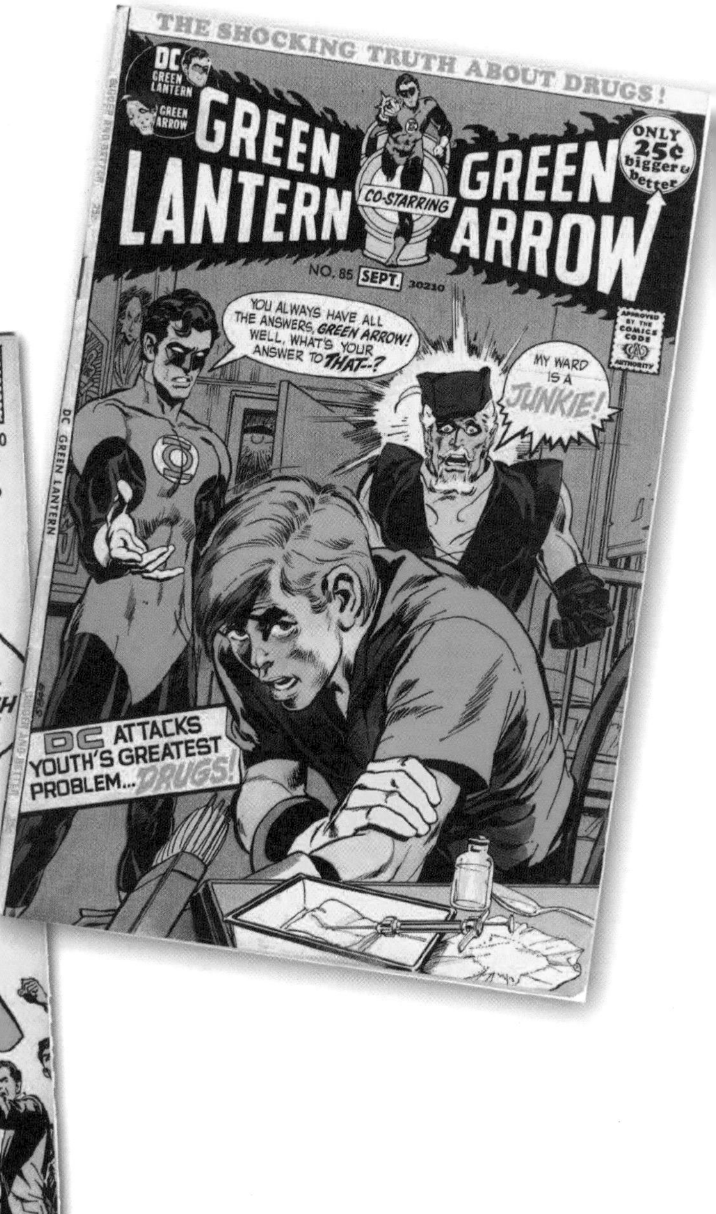
THE SHOCKING TRUTH ABOUT DRUGS!
DC GREEN LANTERN GREEN ARROW
GREEN LANTERN
CO-STARRING
GREEN ARROW
ONLY 25¢ bigger & better
NO. 85 SEPT. 30210
APPROVED BY THE COMICS CODE AUTHORITY
YOU ALWAYS HAVE ALL THE ANSWERS, GREEN ARROW! WELL, WHAT'S YOUR ANSWER TO THAT--?
MY WARD IS A JUNKIE!
DC ATTACKS YOUTH'S GREATEST PROBLEM...DRUGS!

NEAL ADAMS, cover artist
SUPERMAN #240 (DC Comics, July 1971)
Private Collection

NEAL ADAMS, cover artist
GREEN LANTERN/GREEN ARROW #85 (DC Comics, August/September 1971)
Collection of Michael Uslan

AT RIGHT:

NEAL ADAMS
Original art for the cover of GREEN LANTERN/GREEN ARROW #87 (DC Comics, December 1971/January 1972)
Ink on paper
Collection of Scott Williams

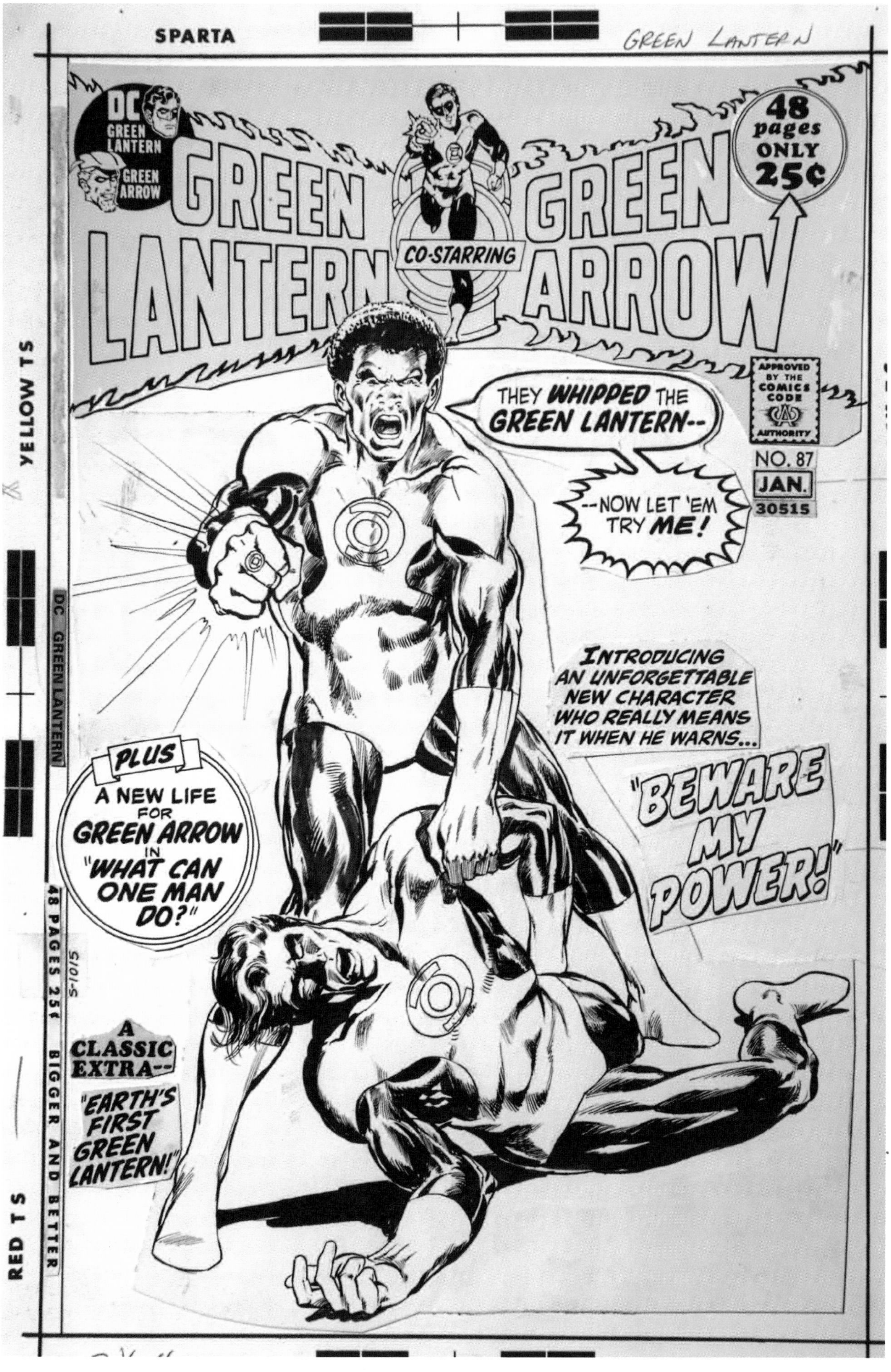
SPARTA
GREEN LANTERN
DC GREEN LANTERN GREEN ARROW
GREEN LANTERN CO-STARRING GREEN ARROW
48 pages ONLY 25¢
APPROVED BY THE COMICS CODE AUTHORITY
NO. 87
JAN.
30515
THEY WHIPPED THE GREEN LANTERN--
--NOW LET 'EM TRY ME!
INTRODUCING AN UNFORGETTABLE NEW CHARACTER WHO REALLY MEANS IT WHEN HE WARNS...
"BEWARE MY POWER!"
PLUS
A NEW LIFE FOR GREEN ARROW IN "WHAT CAN ONE MAN DO?"
A CLASSIC EXTRA--
"EARTH'S FIRST GREEN LANTERN!"
YELLOW TS
DC GREEN LANTERN
48 PAGES 25¢ BIGGER AND BETTER
RED TS
S-1015

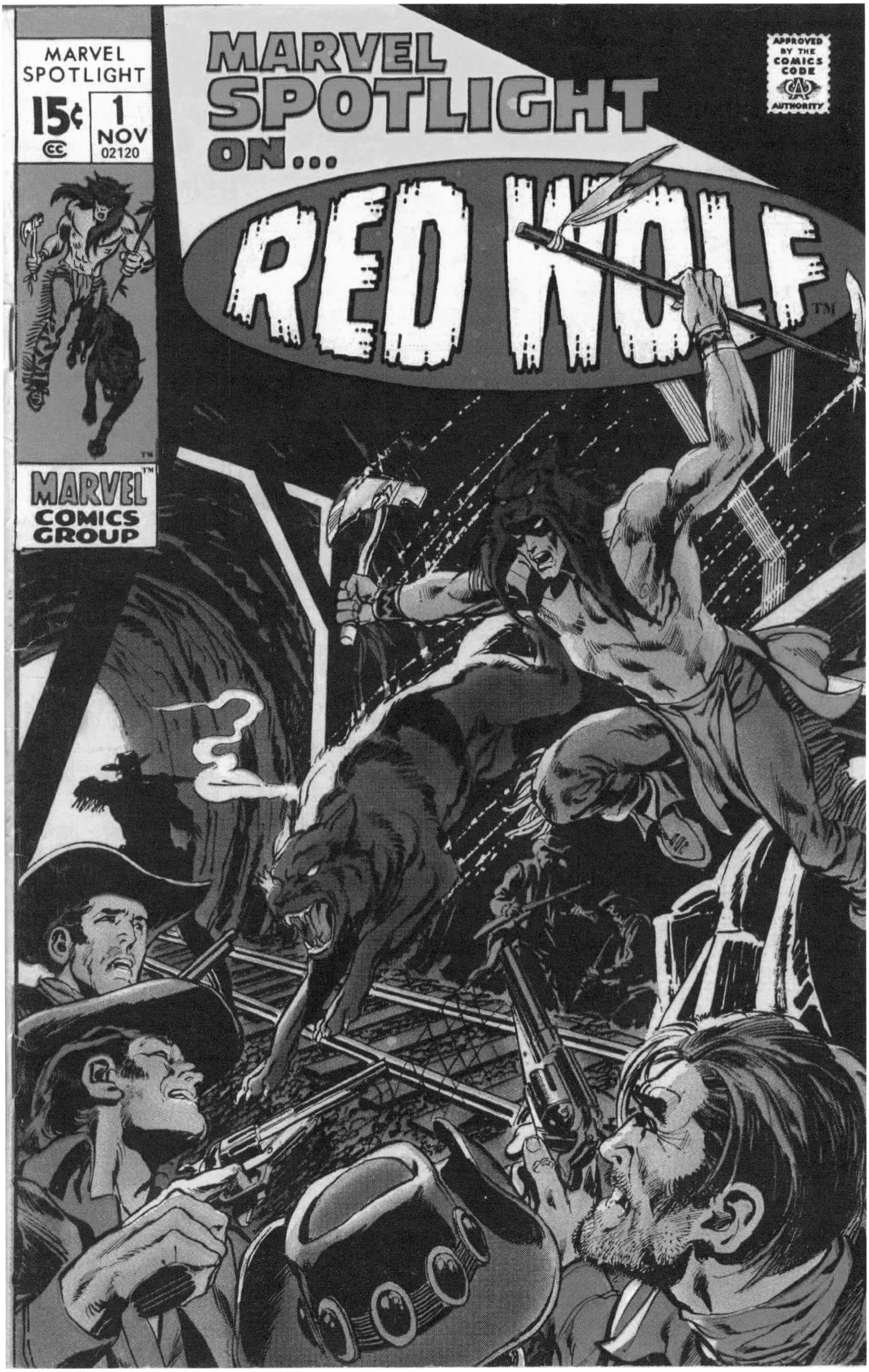
MARVEL SPOTLIGHT
15¢
1
NOV
02120
MARVEL COMICS GROUP
APPROVED BY THE COMICS CODE AUTHORITY
MARVEL SPOTLIGHT ON...
RED WOLF

AMERICAN INDIAN SUPER HEROES:
STEREOTYPES & REALITIES

By TWIG JOHNSON

For years, comic books have addressed social issues in a variety of settings. Unfortunately, much of what has been created perpetuates racial stereotypes. From the earliest portrayals of American Indians in dime store novels that were popular in the late 19th and 20th centuries to *Scalped*, published in 2007, American Indians are often portrayed as savage heathens, noble savages, simple-minded sidekicks, mystical new age shamans, or hopeless people living amidst insurmountable social problems on the reservations.

This bleak picture is changing with Native American artists and tribes using comic books as a way to raise awareness for not only the problems they face, but to tell stories that promote the positive aspects of Native American culture. These are tales that utilize native beliefs and oral traditions to help celebrate and understand what it means to be indigenous. Excellent examples of these are *Darkness Calls* (2006), by Red Earth Media, published by The Healthy Aboriginal Network in British Columbia, and *A Hero's Voice* (2007), by the Mille Lacs Band of Ojibwe that traces the story of the six Ojibwe leaders who have shaped the history of their people.

The concept of super heroes is not a new idea within native culture. For thousands of years the oral traditions of these cultures often talked about beings with the power to generate all of creation, steal the sun, help people to survive cataclysmic events, slay monsters, control the environment, and generally help humanity. Early comic book characters that were based on American Indian themes were usually somehow linked with the natural and supernatural world, and although characterized as indigenous, were in actuality, white men raised by natives. The first truly native character that was created and drawn by non-natives was Marvel's *Red Wolf* (1971), who is the alter ego of Johnny Wakely, a Cheyenne boy who was raised by a white couple in the late 19th century. He used his powers to promote peace between the white and American Indian people. Using stereotypical themes and the appeal of the western genre, *Red Wolf* was a popular comic. In contrast to this early character, the recent comic *Peace Party* (1999) by Rob Schmidt is an attempt to combine the super hero genre with a multicultural character narrative that accurately depicts the lives and heritage of American Indians.

Super heroes have taken on a new identity within indigenous cultures. They are found in the stories of ancient cultures, in everyday life, and in the pages of native comic books whose stories integrate modern life with powerful traditions. These stories compel people to realize that indigenous cultures have both history and a contemporary living presence.

NEAL ADAMS, cover artist
MARVEL SPOTLIGHT #1
(Marvel Comics, November 1971)
Collection of Le Brun Library, Montclair Art Museum

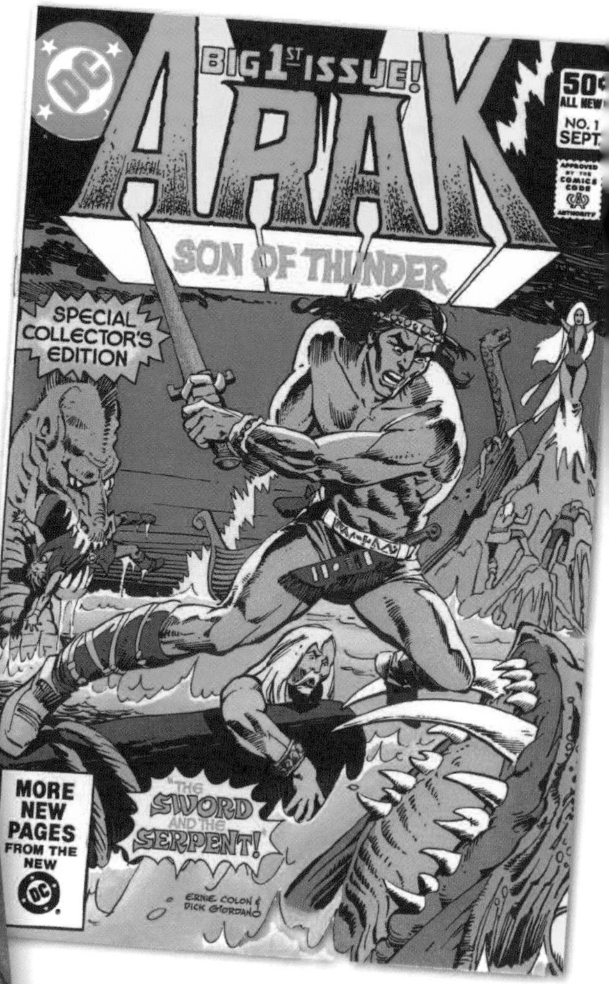
DC
BIG 1ST ISSUE!
ARAK
SON OF THUNDER
50¢
ALL NEW
NO. 1
SEPT
SPECIAL COLLECTOR'S EDITION
MORE NEW PAGES FROM THE NEW DC
"THE SWORD AND THE SERPENT!"
ERNIE COLON & DICK GIORDANO

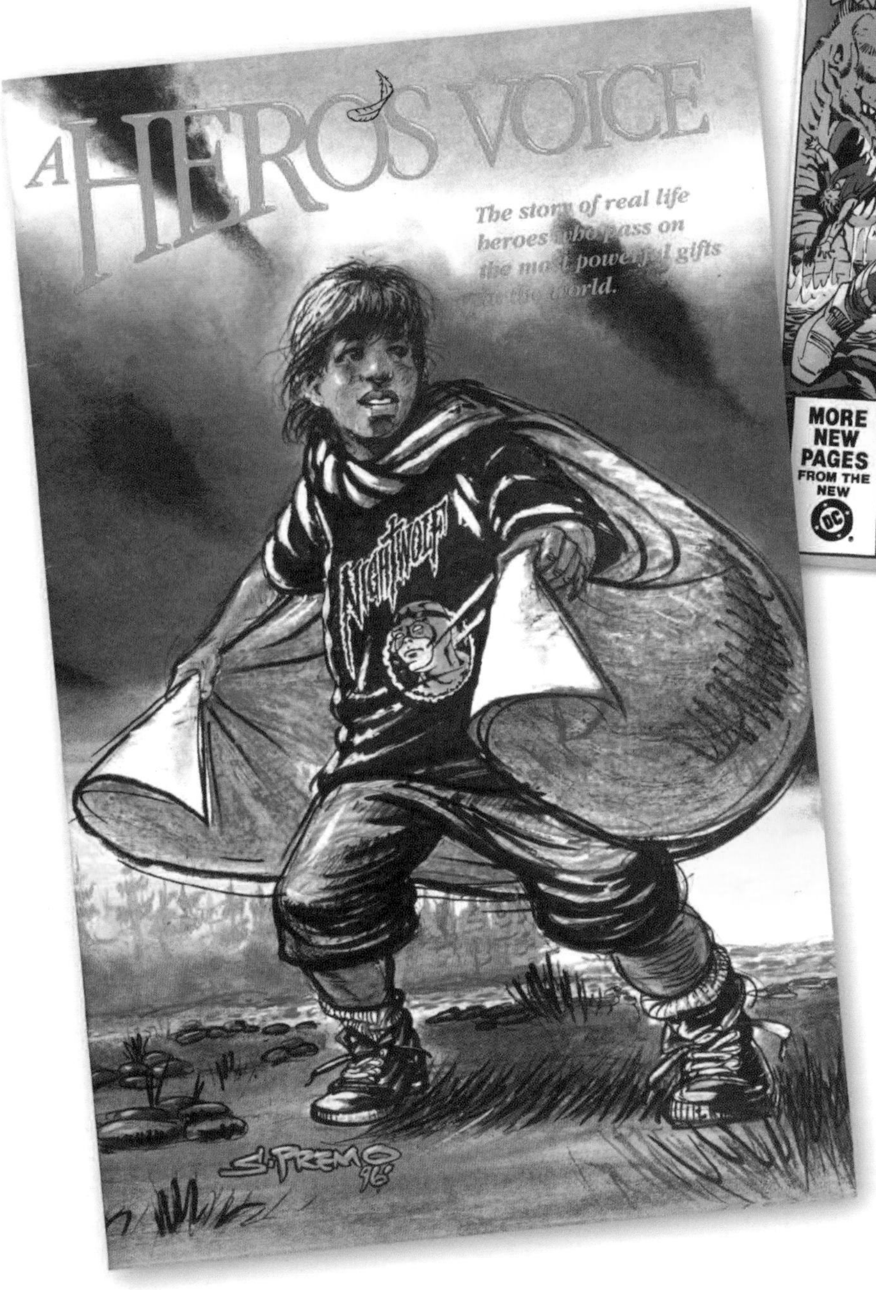
A HERO'S VOICE
S. PREMO 96

ERNIE COLON, cover penciller and DICK GIORDANO, cover inker
***ARAK: SON OF THUNDER #1* (DC Comics, September 1981)**
Collection of Le Brun Library, Montclair Art Museum

STEVE PREMO, cover artist
***A HERO'S VOICE* (The Mille Lacs Band of Ojibwe: Educational Comic Book Series, 1996)**
Collection of Le Brun Library, Montclair Art Museum

AT RIGHT:

DIMI MACHERAS, cover artist
***STRONG MAN #1* (Association of Alaska School Boards, February 2007)**
Collection of Le Brun Library, Montclair Art Museum

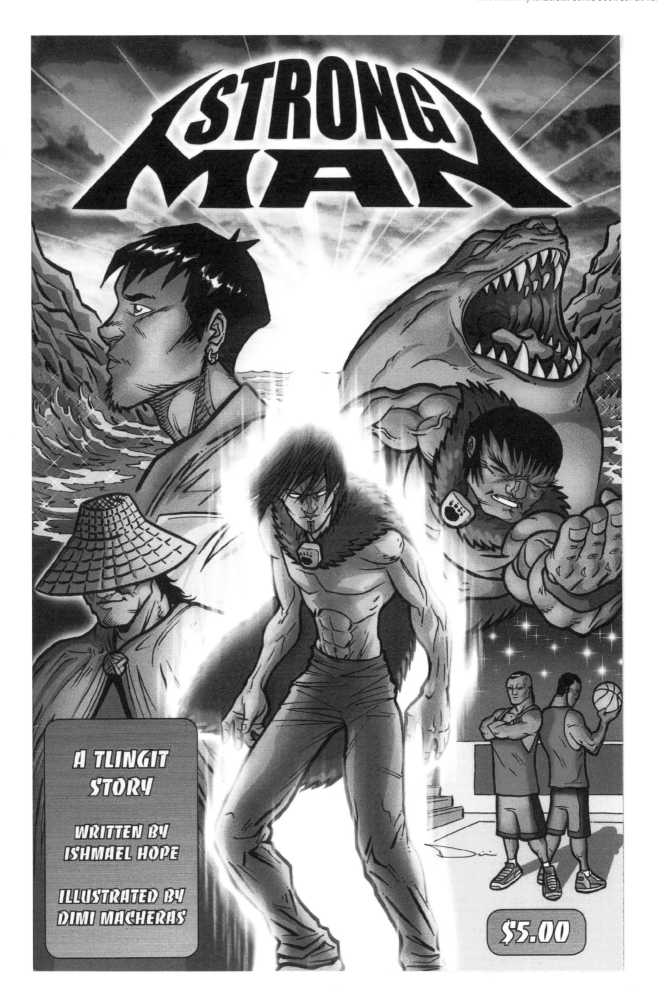

STRONG MAN

A TLINGIT STORY

WRITTEN BY ISHMAEL HOPE

ILLUSTRATED BY DIMI MACHERAS

$5.00

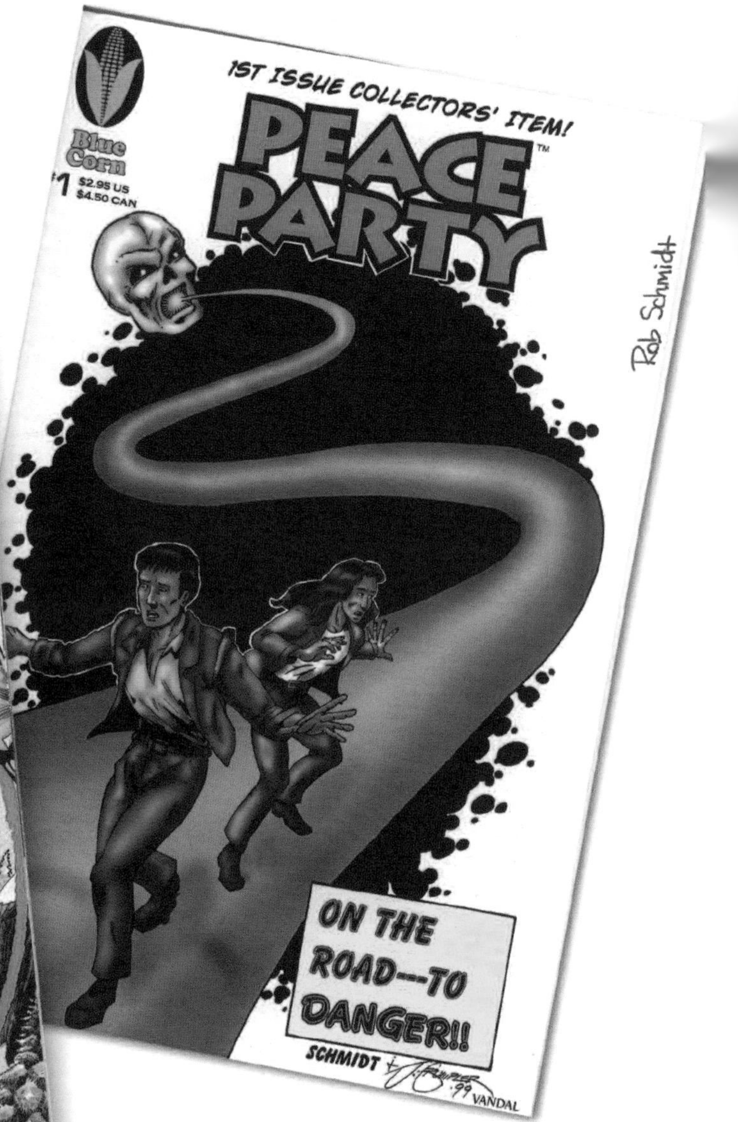
Blue Corn
#1 $2.95 US $4.50 CAN
1ST ISSUE COLLECTORS' ITEM!
PEACE PARTY™
Rob Schmidt
ON THE ROAD---TO DANGER!!
SCHMIDT
'99 VANDAL

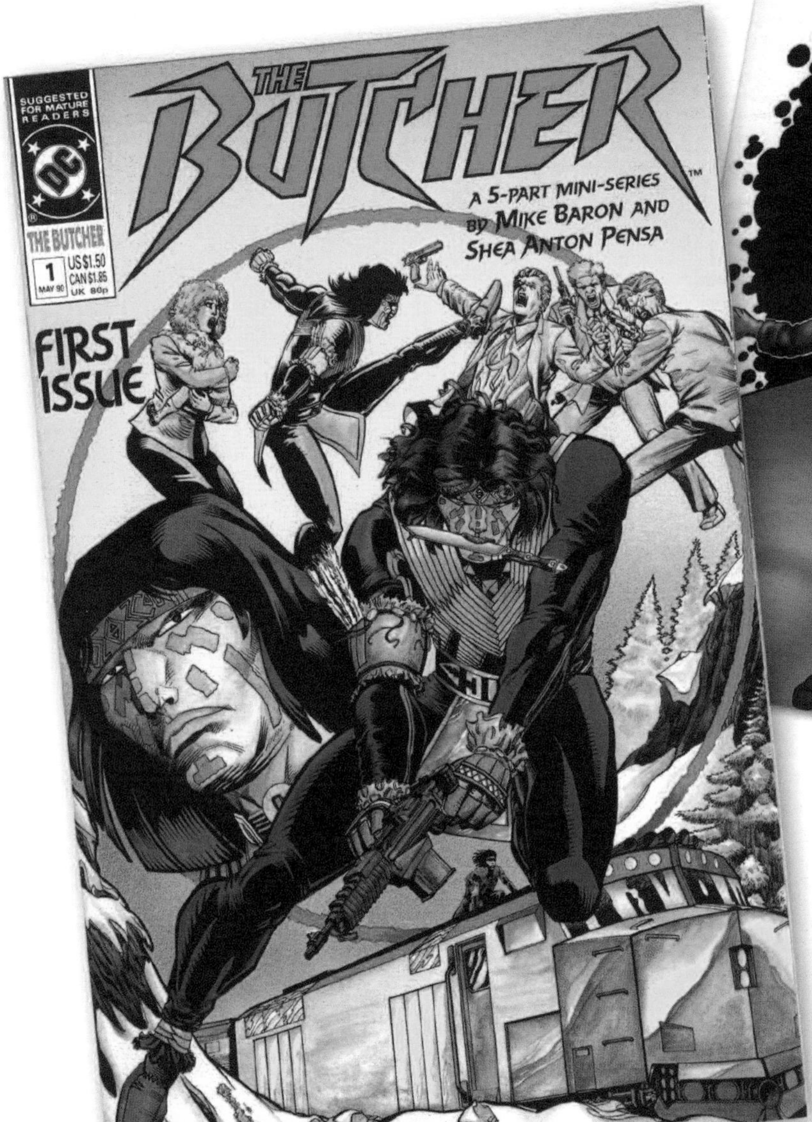
SUGGESTED FOR MATURE READERS
DC
THE BUTCHER
1 US $1.50 CAN $1.85 UK 80p
MAY 90
THE BUTCHER™
A 5-PART MINI-SERIES BY MIKE BARON AND SHEA ANTON PENSA
FIRST ISSUE

***RON FATTORUSO*, cover penciller and *MIKE KELLEHER*, cover inker**
***PEACE PARTY #1* (Blue Corn Comics, 1999)**
Collection of Le Brun Library, Montclair Art Museum

***SHEA ANTON PENSA*, cover artist**
***THE BUTCHER #1* (DC Comics, May 1990)**
Collection of Le Brun Library, Montclair Art Museum

AT RIGHT:

***JOCK*, cover artist**
***SCALPED #1* (Vertigo Comics, an imprint of DC Comics, March 2007)**
Collection of Le Brun Library, Montclair Art Museum

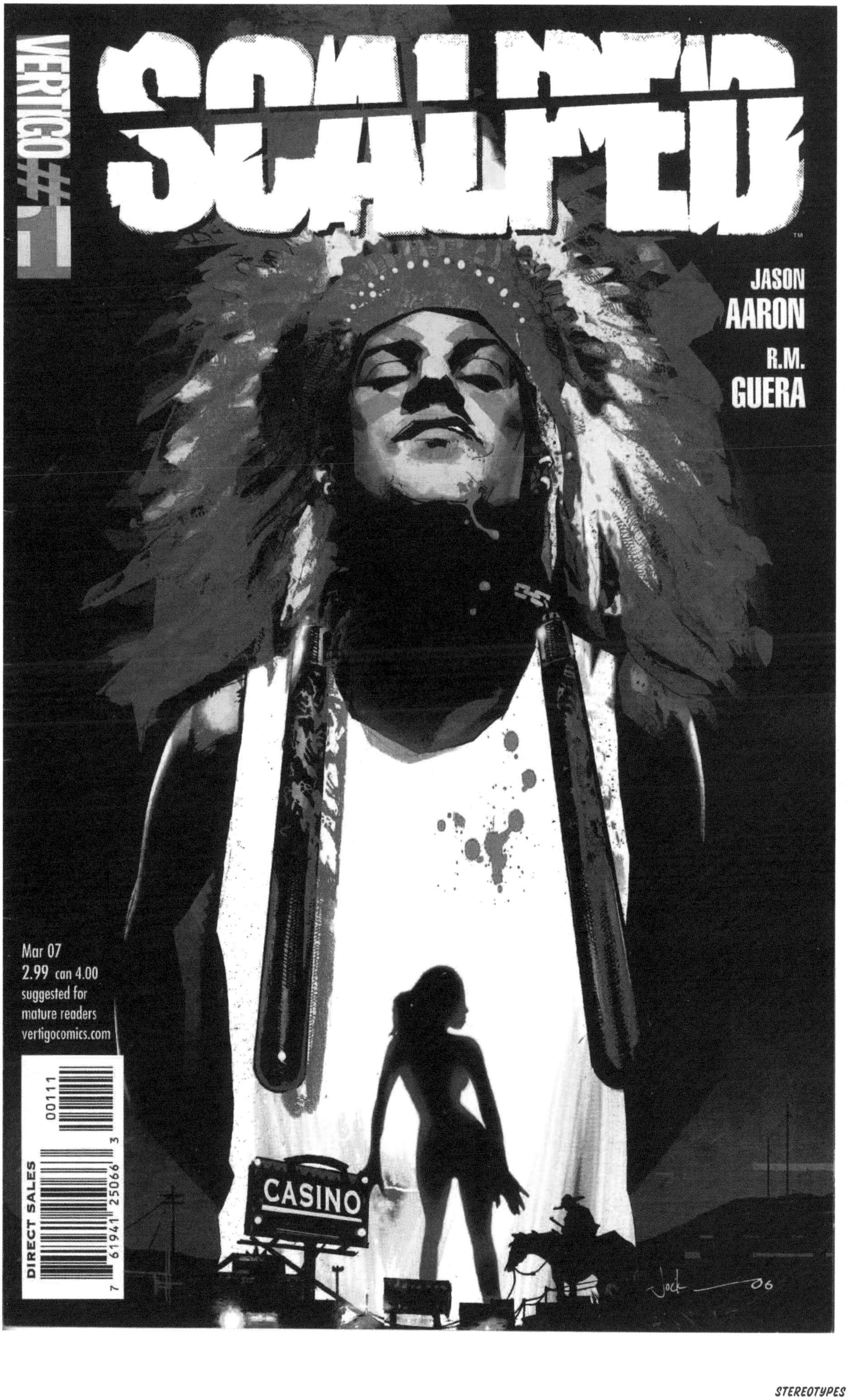
VERTIGO #1
SCALPED™
JASON AARON
R.M. GUERA
Mar 07
2.99 can 4.00
suggested for
mature readers
vertigocomics.com
DIRECT SALES
CASINO

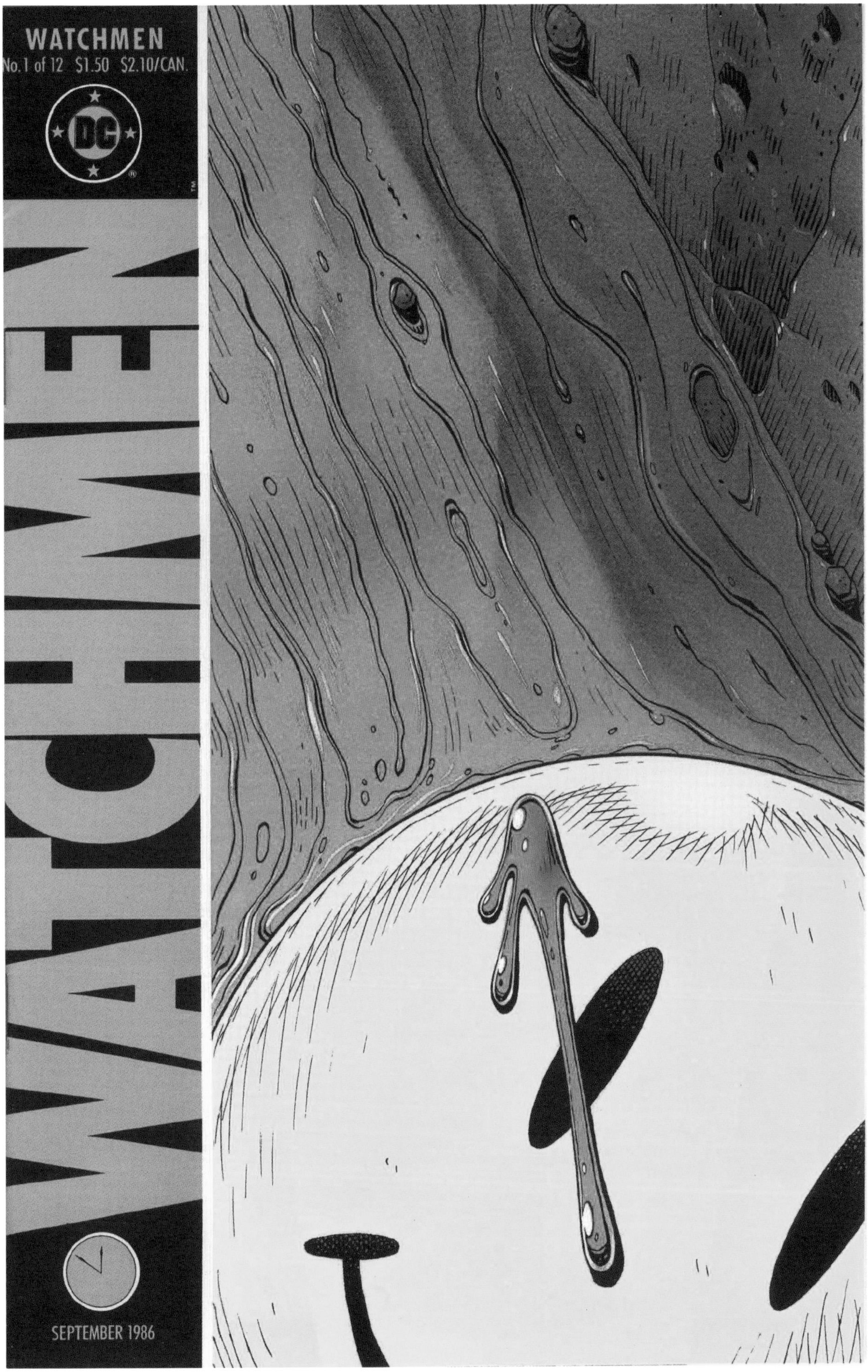
WATCHMEN
No. 1 of 12 $1.50 $2.10/CAN.
DC
WATCHMEN
SEPTEMBER 1986

DIVERSITY AND MORAL COMPLEXITY:
COMIC BOOK SUPER HEROES OF THE 1980s AND 1990s

The restructuring of the comic book industry in the late 1970s and early 80s resulted in the direct marketing of comic books in specialty stores. The institution of creators' rights also encouraged comic book makers to accommodate the taste of the market for super heroes with more realism, violence, cynicism, and moral ambiguity. The industry also had to contend with slumping sales of comics due in part to competition from interactive technology.

To reinvigorate the aging super hero genre, DC issued the epic series *Crisis on Infinite Earths* (1985-86), in order to reintroduce such classic characters as Superman and Supergirl with new origin stories. The temporary death of Superman in January 1993, followed by his multi-issue resurrection and marriage to Lois Lane, focused much media attention on super hero comics. In *Marvel Super-Heroes: Secret Wars* (1984), Marvel teamed up all of its super heroes and introduced a new black costume for Spider-Man. ✓

Batman experienced a major resurgence as an older and slightly mad right-wing moralist in Frank Miller's gritty, four issue series *Batman: The Dark Knight Returns* (DC Comics, 1986), which was published as a graphic novel and expanded the notion of comic books as literature. This story was responsible for the rejuvenation of Batman as a dark character, whose renewed popularity culminated in the series of blockbuster Warner films.

During this era the most complex and ambitious super hero series, *Watchmen*, was published by DC as a 12-issue series and then as a graphic novel. Featuring super heroes as real, flawed individuals largely lacking in superpowers, Alan Moore's and Dave Gibbon's *Watchmen* was a highly influential deconstruction of the conventional super hero archetype.

The comic book industry was also expanded with the launching in 1992 of Milestone Comics (a division of DC) by Denys Cowan, Dwayne McDuffie, and other African American creators who wanted to provide sorely needed models of black heroism. Although no longer in existence, Milestone enriched the super hero genre with such memorable characters as Static, a geeky high school student with a bizarre array of electrical powers. ✓

DAVE GIBBONS, cover artist
WATCHMEN #1 (DC Comics, September 1986)
Collection of Rich Sheinaus

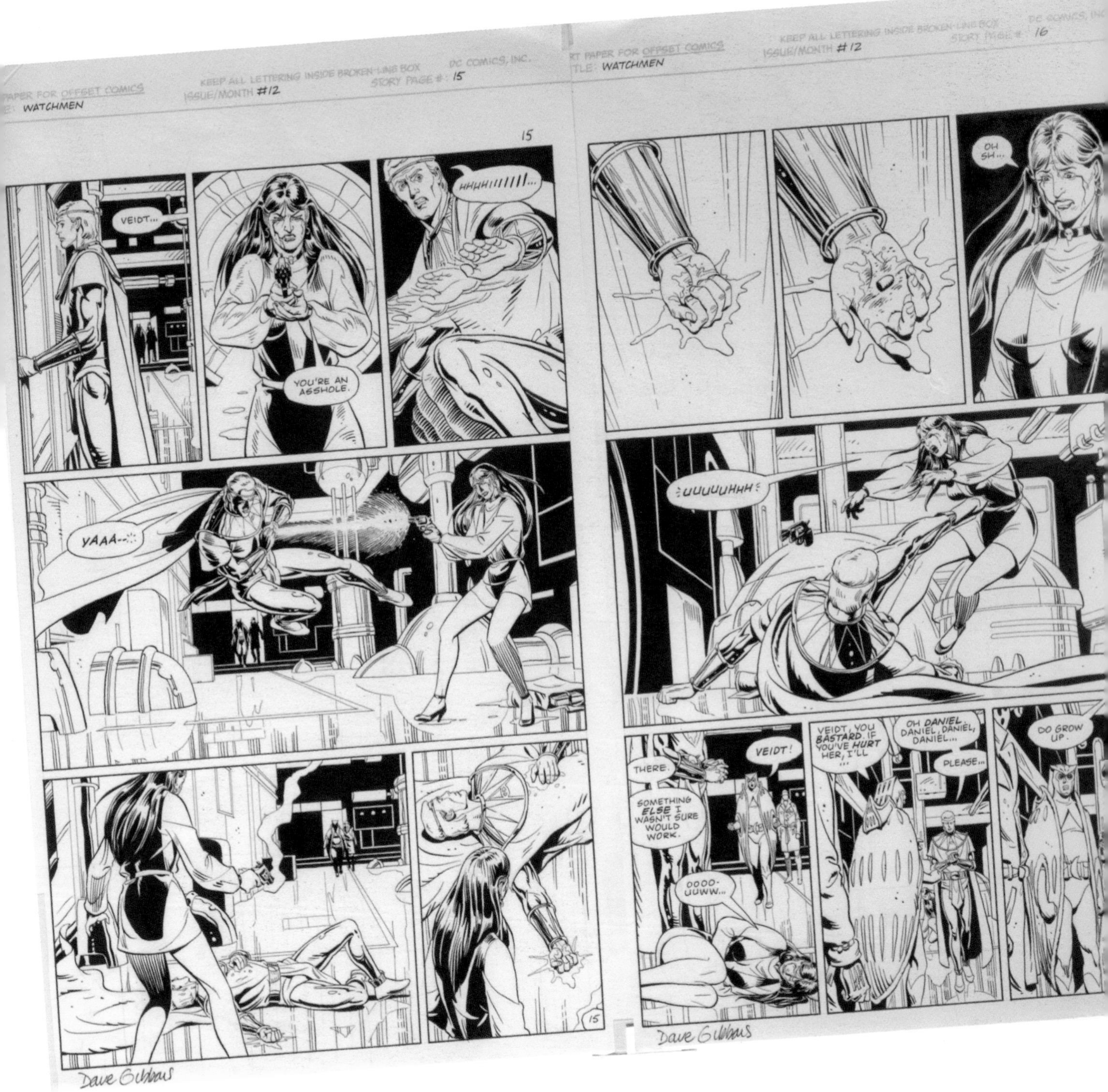
KEEP ALL LETTERING INSIDE BROKEN-LINE BOX
DC COMICS, INC.
WATCHMEN
ISSUE/MONTH #12
STORY PAGE #: 15
15
VEIDT...
YOU'RE AN ASSHOLE.
YAAA--
15
Dave Gibbons
KEEP ALL LETTERING INSIDE BROKEN-LINE BOX
WATCHMEN
ISSUE/MONTH #12
STORY PAGE #: 16
OH SH...
UUUUUHHH
THERE.
SOMETHING ELSE I WASN'T SURE WOULD WORK.
VEIDT!
OOOO-UUWW...
VEIDT, YOU BASTARD. IF YOU'VE HURT HER, I'LL ...
OH DANIEL. DANIEL, DANIEL, DANIEL...
PLEASE...
DO GROW UP.
Dave Gibbons

DAVE GIBBONS
Original art for double page spread in WATCHMEN #1
(DC Comics, October 1987)
Pen and ink on paper
Collection of Srihari S. Naidu, M.D.

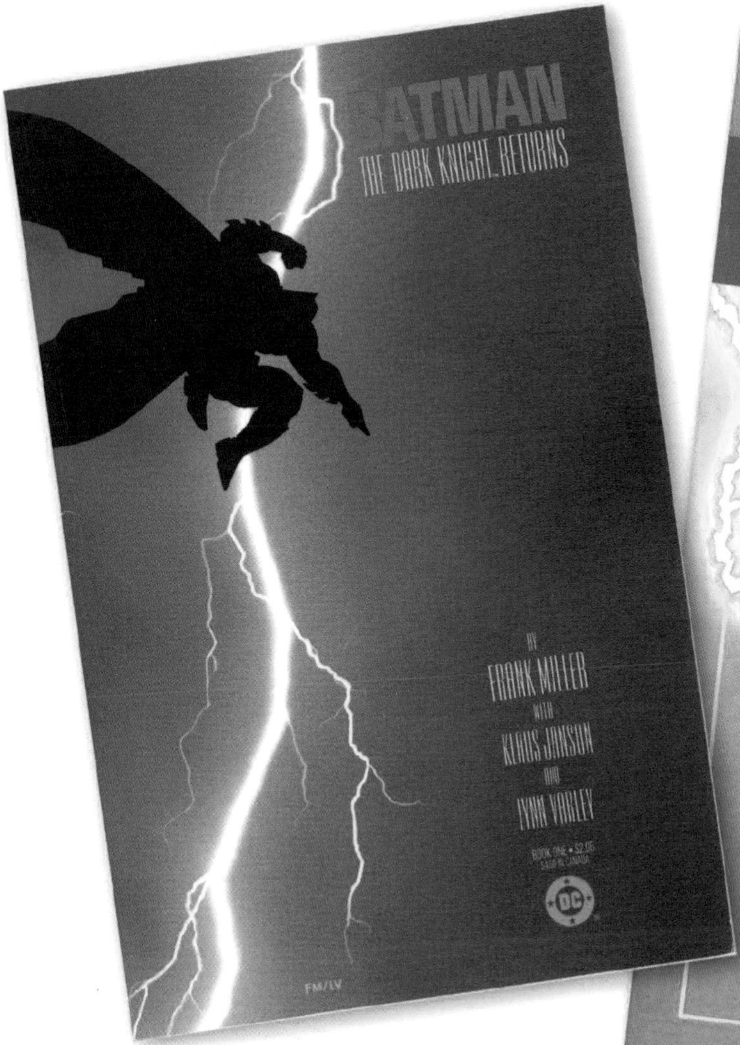
BATMAN
THE DARK KNIGHT RETURNS
BY
FRANK MILLER
WITH
KLAUS JANSON
AND
LYNN VARLEY

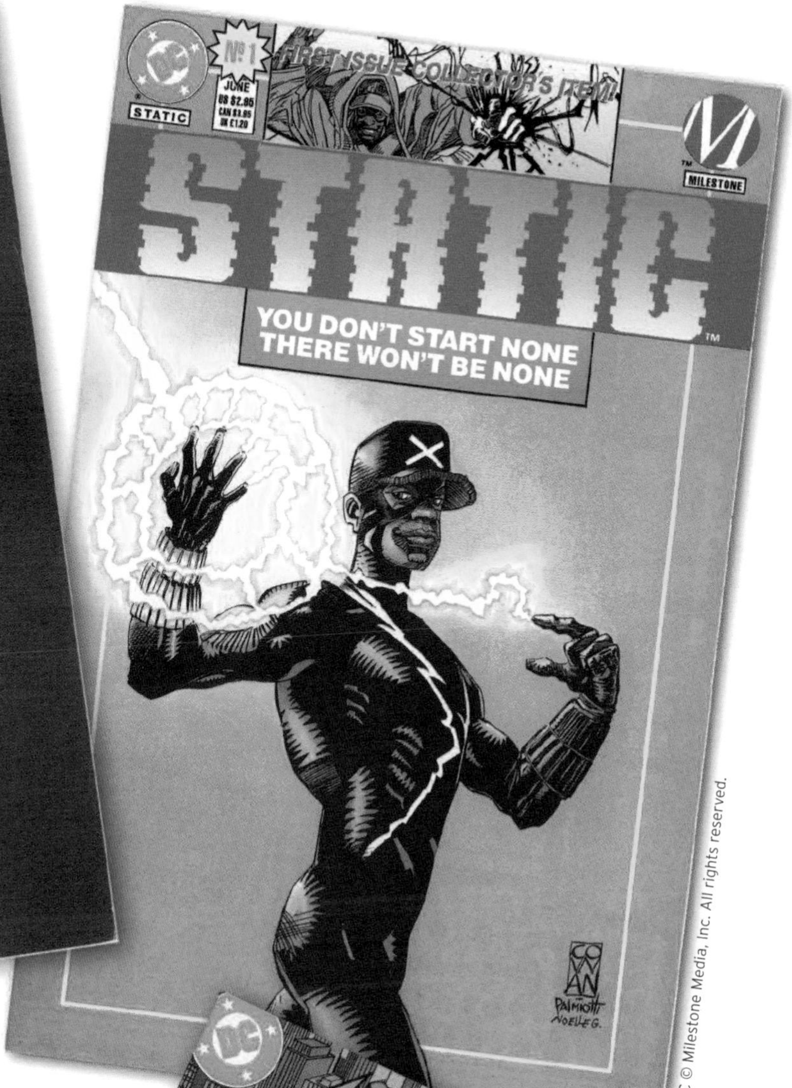
No 1
FIRST ISSUE COLLECTOR'S ITEM!
STATIC
MILESTONE
STATIC
YOU DON'T START NONE
THERE WON'T BE NONE

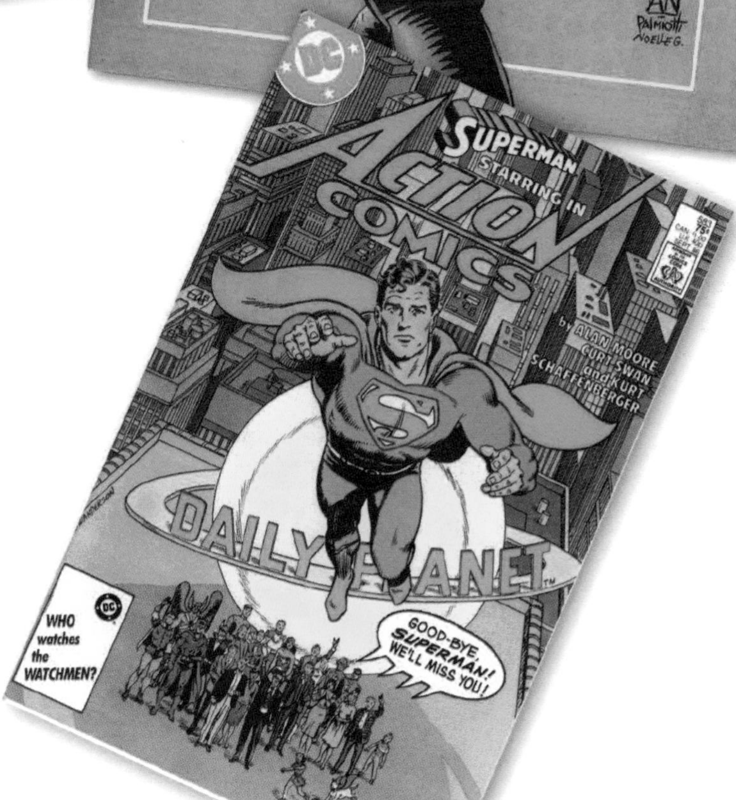
SUPERMAN
STARRING IN
ACTION COMICS
by ALAN MOORE
CURT SWAN
and KURT
SCHAFFENBERGER
DAILY PLANET
WHO watches the WATCHMEN?
GOOD-BYE, SUPERMAN! WE'LL MISS YOU!

***FRANK MILLER*, cover penciller and writer**
***KLAUS JANSON*, cover inker**
***BATMAN: THE DARK KNIGHT RETURNS*, Book One**
(DC Comics, 1986)
Collection of Rich Sheinaus

***DENYS COWAN*, cover penciller and**
***JIMMY PALMIOTTI*, cover inker**
STATIC #1 (Milestone, a division of DC Comics,
June 1993)
Collection of Rich Sheinaus

***CURT SWAN*, cover penciller and**
***MURPHY ANDERSON*, cover inker**
ACTION COMICS #583 (DC Comics, September 1986)
Private Collection

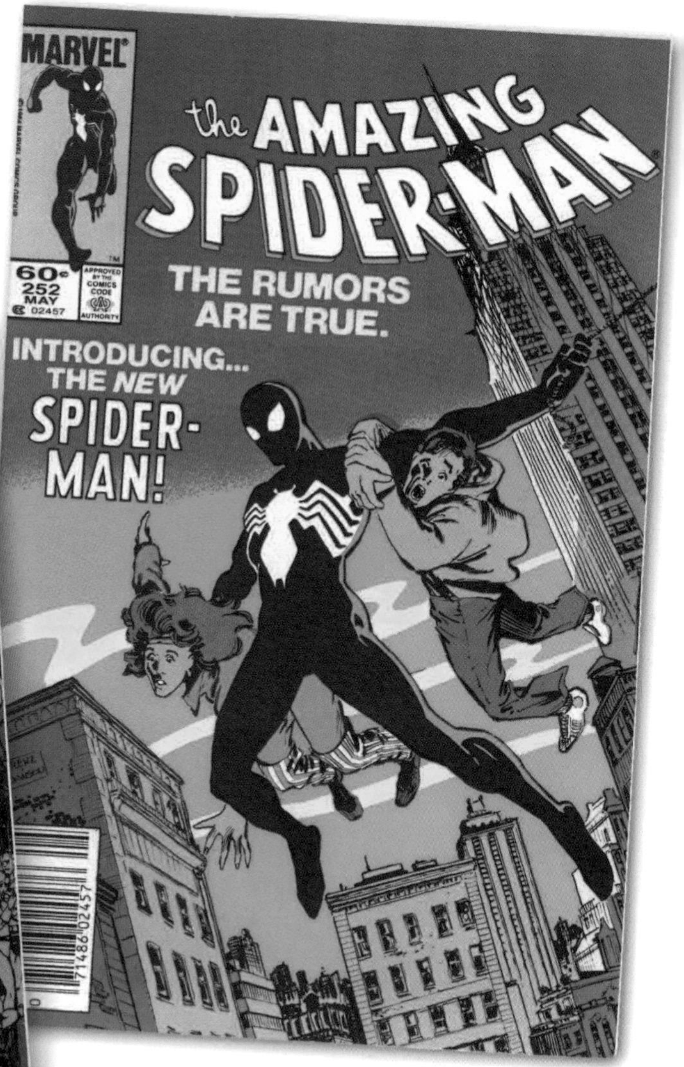
MARVEL
the AMAZING SPIDER-MAN
60¢
252
MAY
THE RUMORS ARE TRUE.
INTRODUCING... THE NEW SPIDER-MAN!

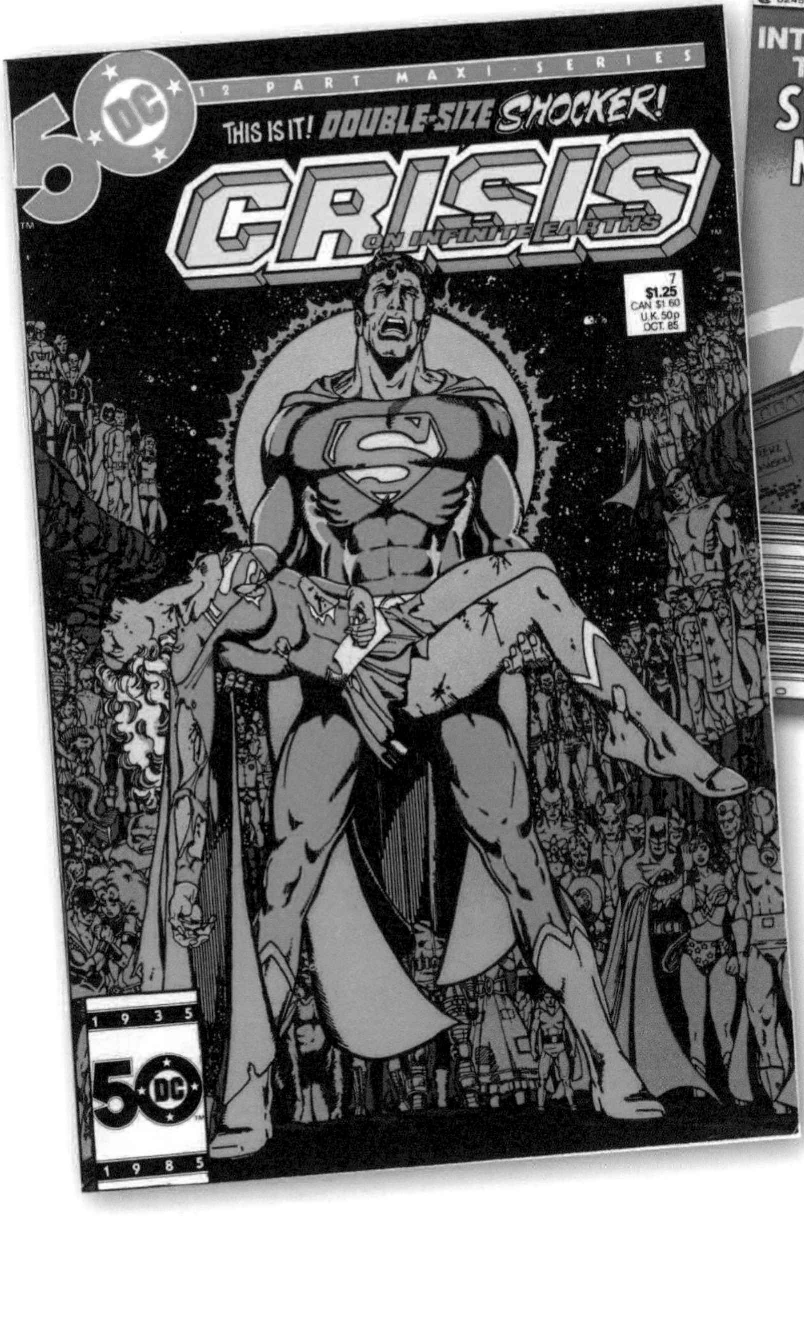
12 PART MAXI-SERIES
THIS IS IT! DOUBLE-SIZE SHOCKER!
CRISIS
ON INFINITE EARTHS
7
$1.25
CAN $1.60
U.K. 50p
OCT. 85
1935
1985

GEORGE PEREZ
CRISIS ON INFINITE EARTHS #7 (DC Comics, October 1985)
Collection of Rich Sheinaus

RON FRENZ, cover artist
SPIDER-MAN #252 (Marvel Comics, May 1984)
Collection of Rich Sheinaus

AT RIGHT:

DAN JURGENS, cover penciller and BRETT BREEDING, cover inker
SUPERMAN #76 (February 1993)
Private collection

DAN JURGENS, cover penciller and BRETT BREEDING, cover inker
Original art for cover of SUPERMAN #76 (DC Comics, February 1993)
Pen and ink on paper
Collection of Srihari S. Naidu, M.D.

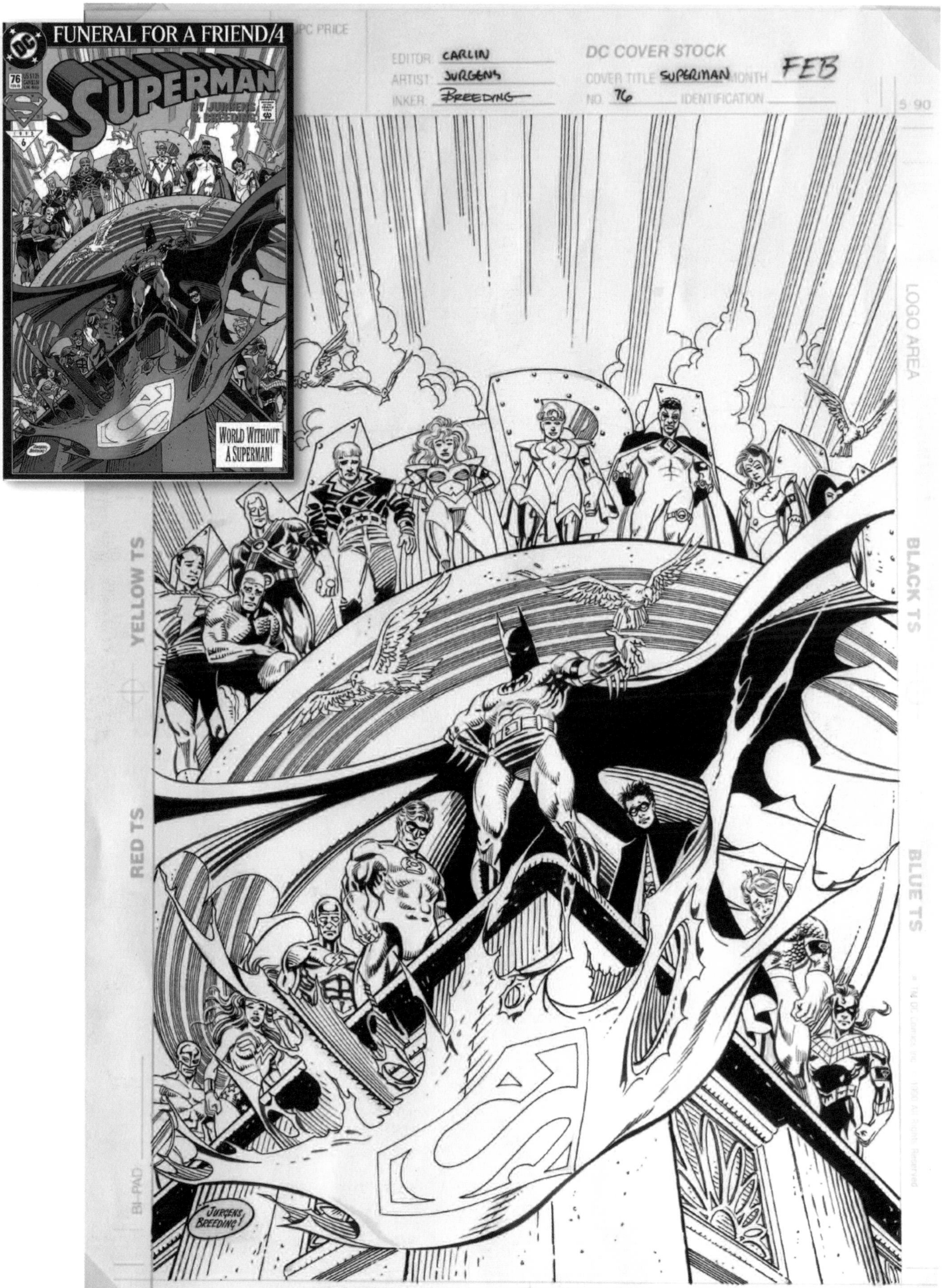
FUNERAL FOR A FRIEND/4
76
SUPERMAN
BY JURGENS & BREEDING
WORLD WITHOUT A SUPERMAN!
JURGENS BREEDING
UPC PRICE
EDITOR CARLIN
ARTIST JURGENS
INKER BREEDING
DC COVER STOCK
COVER TITLE SUPERMAN MONTH FEB
NO. 76 IDENTIFICATION
5/90
LOGO AREA
YELLOW TS
BLACK TS
RED TS
BLUE TS
BI-PAD
JURGENS BREEDING!

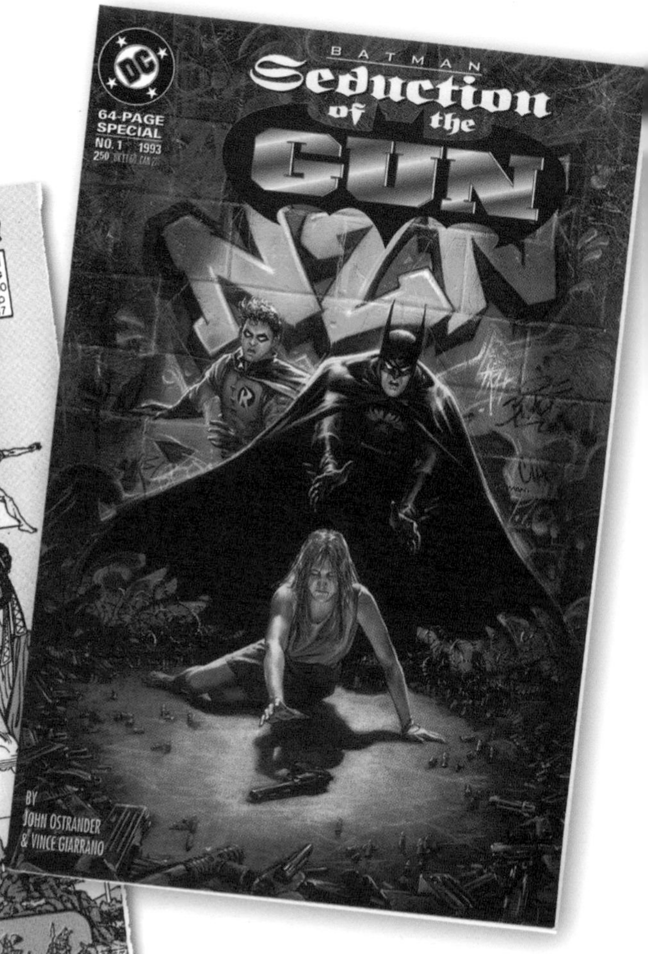
BATMAN
Seduction of the GUN
64-PAGE SPECIAL
NO. 1 1993
BY
JOHN OSTRANDER
& VINCE GIARRANO

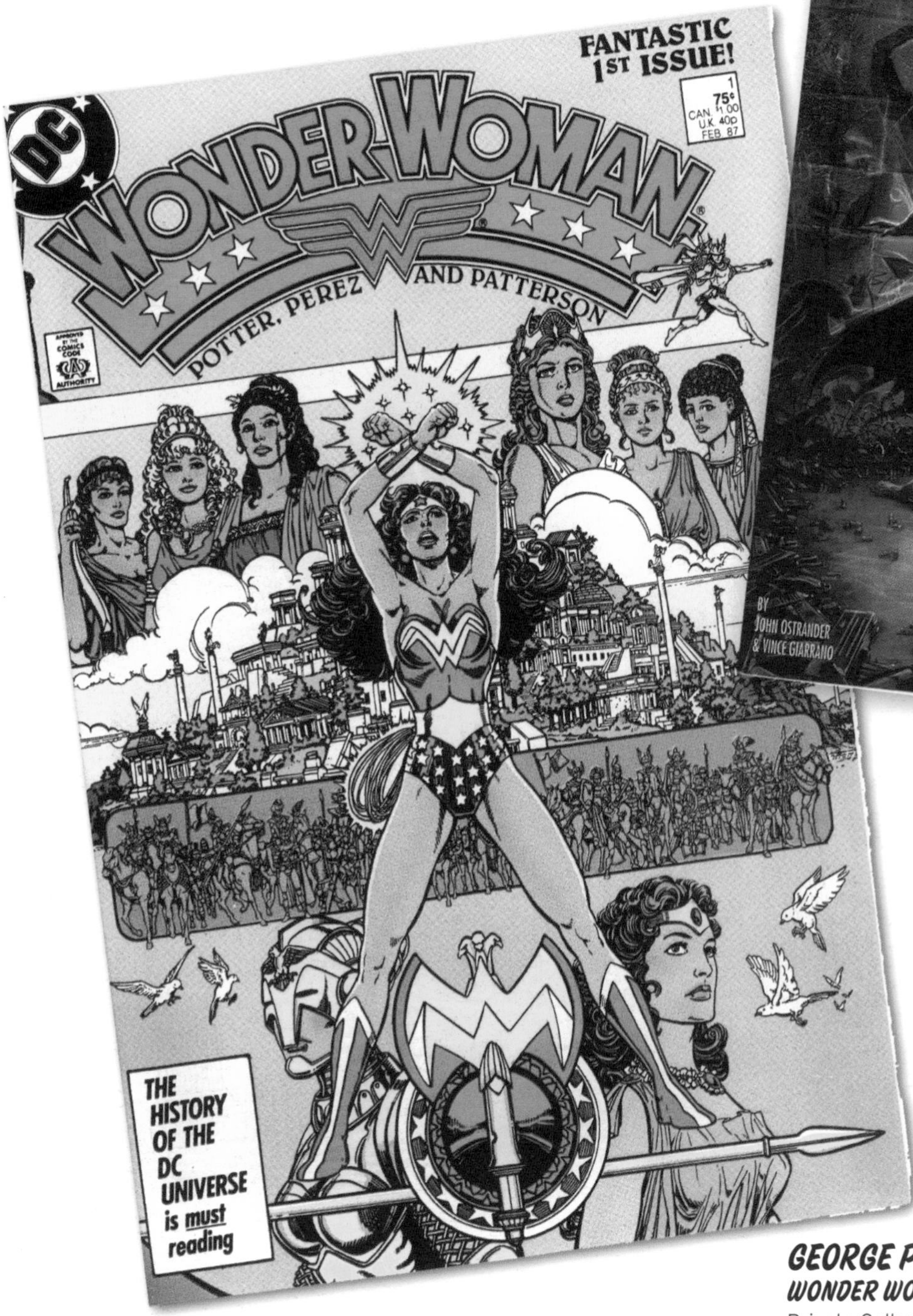
FANTASTIC 1ST ISSUE!
1
75¢
CAN. 1.00
U.K. 40p
FEB. 87
WONDER WOMAN
POTTER, PEREZ AND PATTERSON
THE HISTORY OF THE DC UNIVERSE is must reading

GEORGE PEREZ, cover artist
WONDER WOMAN (vol. 2) #1 (DC Comics, February 1987)
Private Collection

DAVE DORMAN, cover artist
BATMAN - SEDUCTION OF THE GUN #1
(DC Comics, February 1993)
Private Collection

AT RIGHT:

DAVE COCKRUM
Original art for splash page for THE UNCANNY X-MEN #147
(MARVEL COMICS, July 1981)
Pen and ink on paper
Collection of Srihari S. Naidu, M.D.

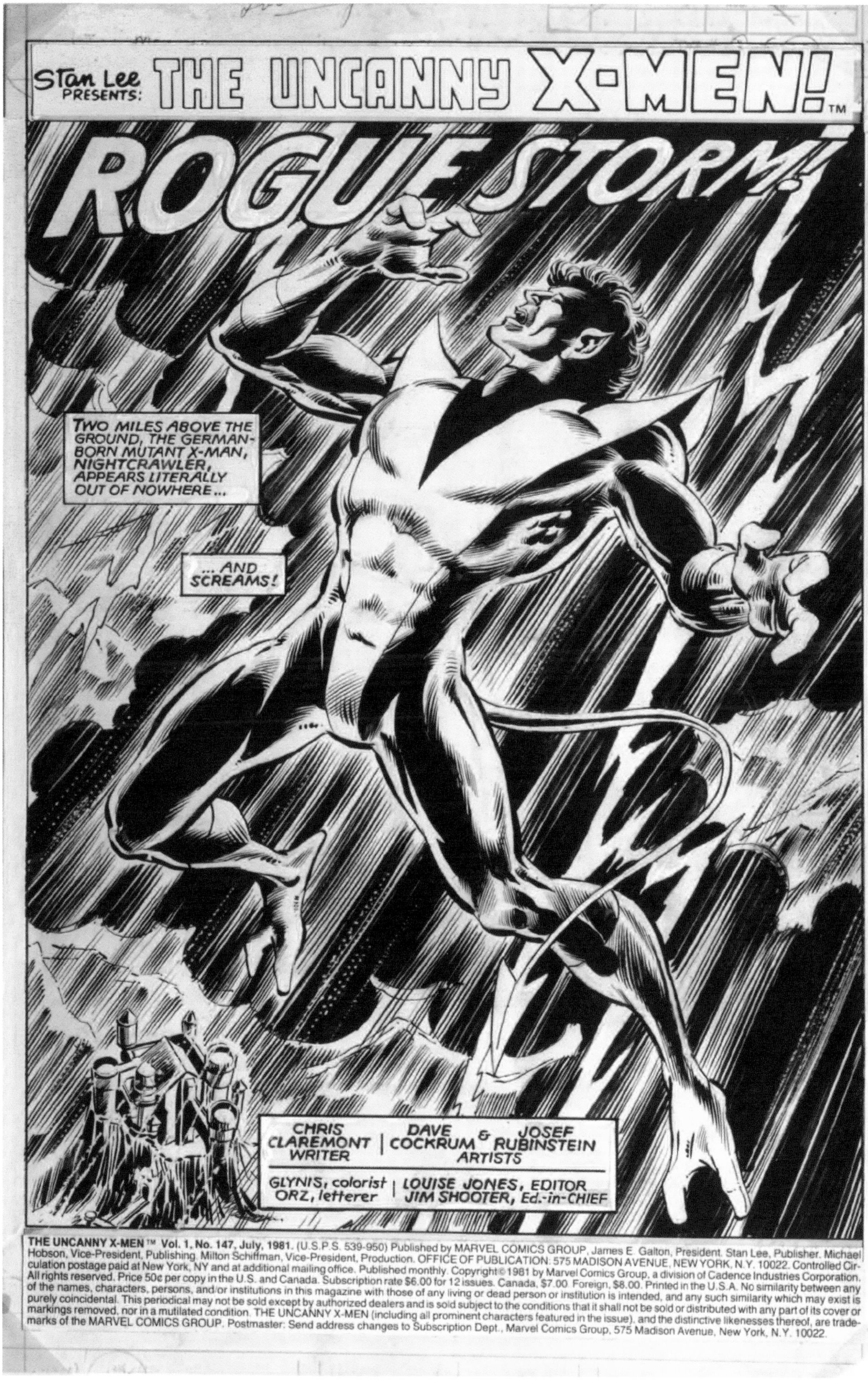
Stan Lee PRESENTS: THE UNCANNY X-MEN! TM
ROGUE STORM!
TWO MILES ABOVE THE GROUND, THE GERMAN-BORN MUTANT X-MAN, NIGHTCRAWLER, APPEARS LITERALLY OUT OF NOWHERE...
...AND SCREAMS!
CHRIS CLAREMONT WRITER | DAVE COCKRUM & JOSEF RUBINSTEIN ARTISTS
GLYNIS, colorist ORZ, letterer | LOUISE JONES, EDITOR JIM SHOOTER, Ed.-in-CHIEF
THE UNCANNY X-MEN™ Vol. 1, No. 147, July, 1981. (U.S.P.S. 539-950) Published by MARVEL COMICS GROUP, James E. Galton, President. Stan Lee, Publisher. Michael Hobson, Vice-President, Publishing. Milton Schiffman, Vice-President, Production. OFFICE OF PUBLICATION: 575 MADISON AVENUE, NEW YORK, N.Y. 10022. Controlled Circulation postage paid at New York, NY and at additional mailing office. Published monthly. Copyright © 1981 by Marvel Comics Group, a division of Cadence Industries Corporation. All rights reserved. Price 50¢ per copy in the U.S. and Canada. Subscription rate $6.00 for 12 issues. Canada, $7.00. Foreign, $8.00. Printed in the U.S.A. No similarity between any of the names, characters, persons, and/or institutions in this magazine with those of any living or dead person or institution is intended, and any such similarity which may exist is purely coincidental. This periodical may not be sold except by authorized dealers and is sold subject to the conditions that it shall not be sold or distributed with any part of its cover or markings removed, nor in a mutilated condition. THE UNCANNY X-MEN (including all prominent characters featured in the issue), and the distinctive likenesses thereof, are trademarks of the MARVEL COMICS GROUP. Postmaster: Send address changes to Subscription Dept., Marvel Comics Group, 575 Madison Avenue, New York, N.Y. 10022.

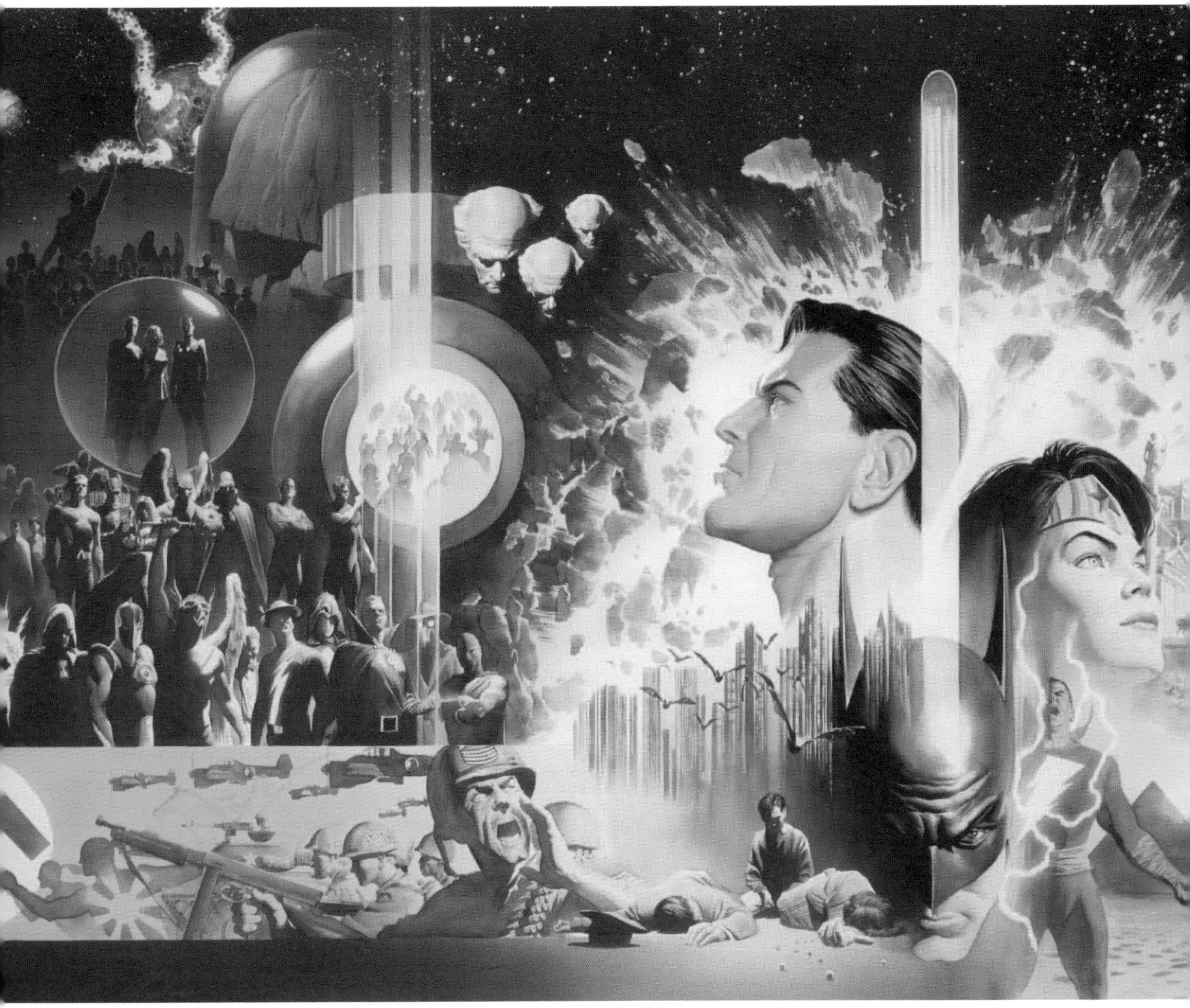

ALEX ROSS
Original art related to the cover of HISTORY OF THE DC UNIVERSE, (DC Comics, 1986), 2002
Mixed media on paper
Collection of Ankur and Indu Jetley

AT RIGHT:

GREG AND TIM HILDEBRANDT
CAPTAIN AMERICA, 1994
Acrylic on board
Collection of Michael Uslan

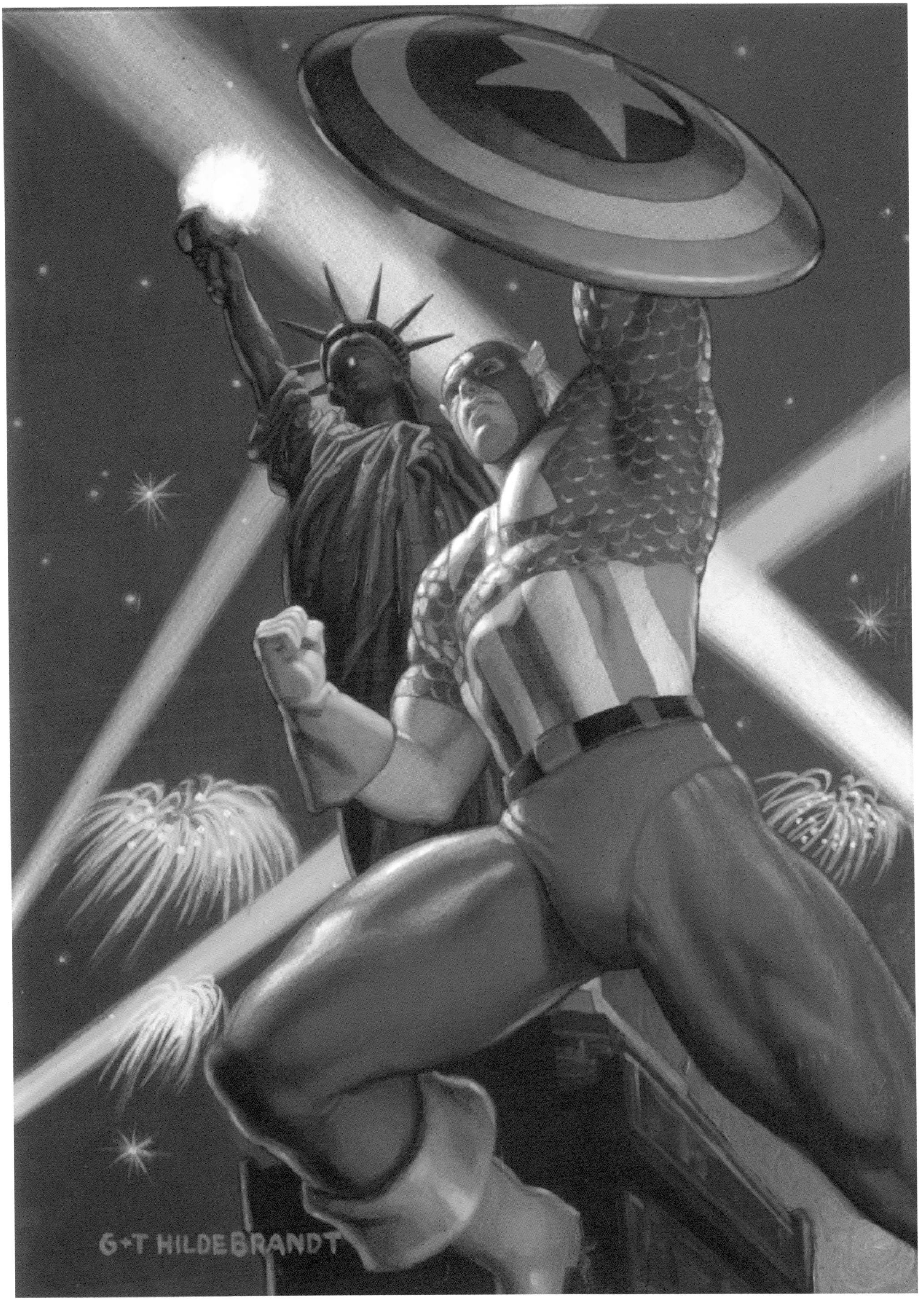
G+T HILDEBRANDT

SUPER HEROES AT GROUND ZERO:
THE NEW CENTURY

Super heroes had responded to national disasters before, yet none that had ever hit so close to home as the tragic events of September 11, 2001. The December 2001 issue of *The Amazing Spider-Man*, encased in a solid black cover, was the first to do so, featuring Spider-Man, Captain America, and Daredevil helping to clear the wreckage in the aftermath of the attacks. Bemoaning their inability to "see it coming...[and] stop it," they stand, on the last page, behind the real heroes—the firefighters, rescue workers, police, and armed forces.

The contemporary reality of a country that inspired cynicism, irony, and moral relativism among its comic book readers inspired some industry members to reevaluate the role of comics in American culture and society. Anxiety about the new century and the election of George Bush had already been reflected in such comics as *President Luthor: Secret Files & Origins* #1 (DC Comics, March 2001) and continued in such comics as *Justice League of America* #83 (DC Comics, September 2003) in which super heroes question President Lex Luthor's decision to unilaterally invade the fictional country of Qurac without evidence of weapons of mass destruction.

In the recent Marvel series, *Civil War*, America's super heroes have been divided against each other in the wake of a tragedy caused by a TV reality show and the government's subsequent requirement that all costumed super heroes unmask themselves and enlist as registered defenders of the country—thus challenging both their rights to privacy and the definition of super heroes. In the April 2007 epilogue issue, the murder of Captain America, characterized as "The Death of the Dream," was a cliffhanger event widely covered in mass media. It provokes questions as to whether comic book super heroes can continue to embody escapism, fantasy, and social relevance in this terrifying post-9-11 world. Still functioning for many readers as metaphors of our dreams and transformative aspirations, they are needed, perhaps now more than ever before.

ALEX ROSS, *cover artist*
THE WORLD'S FINEST COMIC BOOK WRITERS & ARTISTS TELL STORIES TO REMEMBER 9-11 SEPTEMBER 11TH 2001 (DC Comics, 2002)
Private Collection

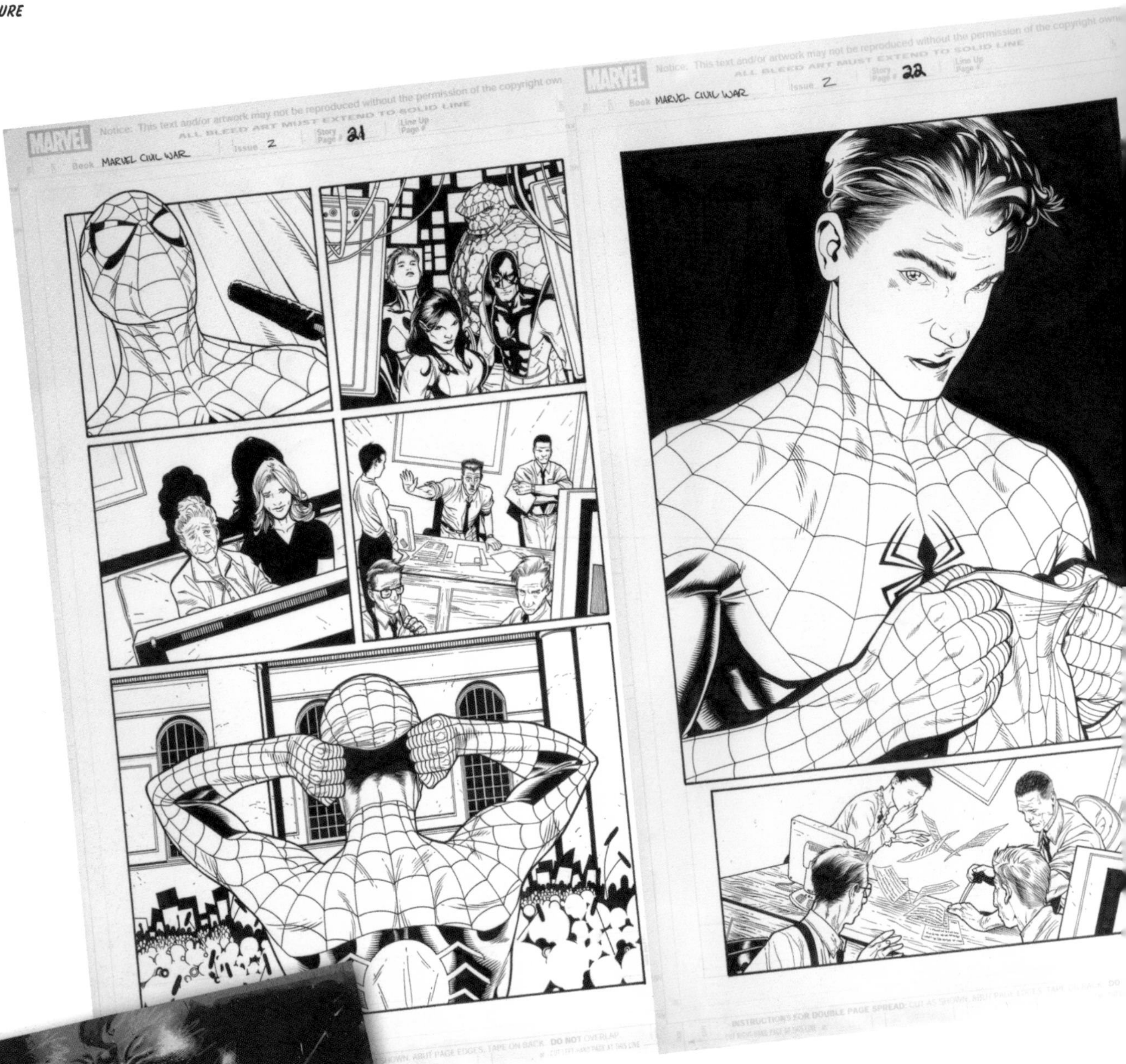
MARVEL
Notice: This text and/or artwork may not be reproduced without the permission of the copyright own
ALL BLEED ART MUST EXTEND TO SOLID LINE
Book MARVEL CIVIL WAR
Issue 2
Story Page # 21
Line Up Page #
MARVEL
Notice: This text and/or artwork may not be reproduced without the permission of the copyright owne
ALL BLEED ART MUST EXTEND TO SOLID LINE
Book MARVEL CIVIL WAR
Issue 2
Story Page # 22
Line Up Page #

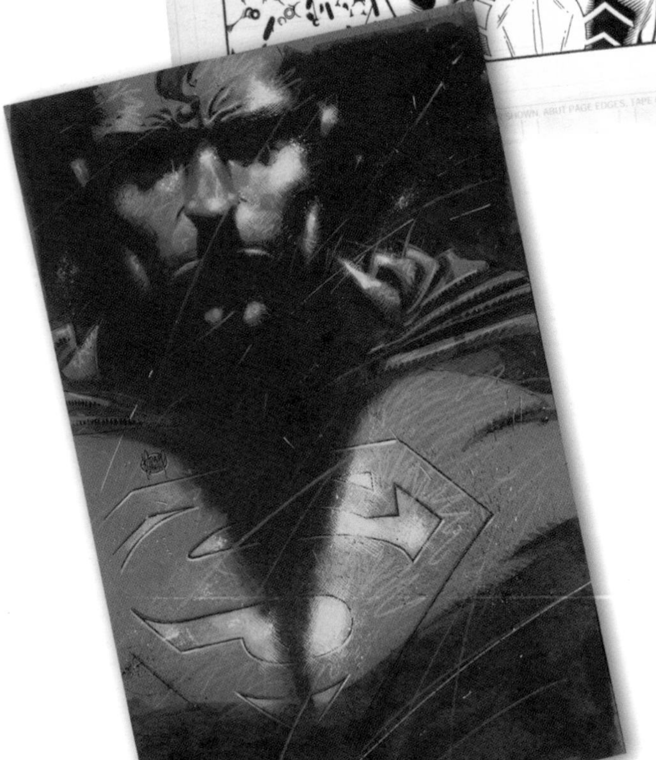

STEVE McNIVEN

Original art for interior pages of CIVIL WAR #2 (Marvel Comics, August 2006)

Pen and ink on Marvel Comics Bristol board
Collection of Steve McNiven

ADAM KUBERT

Original art for the cover of ACTION COMICS #844 (DC Comics, December 2006)

Ink and gouache on cardboard
Collection of the artist

AT RIGHT:

STEVE EPTING, cover artist

CAPTAIN AMERICA (Civil War Epilogue) #25 (Marvel Comics, April 2007)

Private Collection

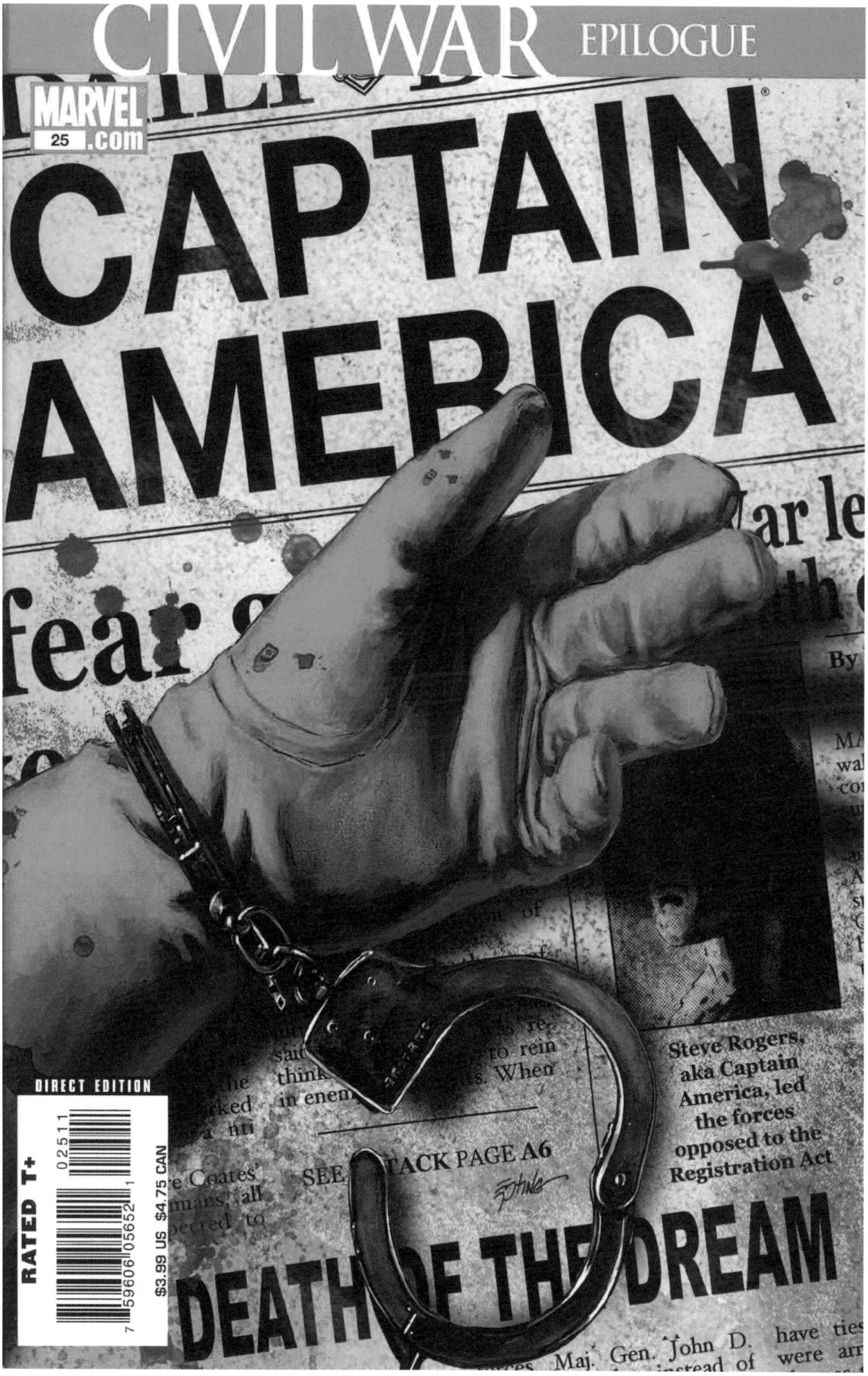
CIVIL WAR
EPILOGUE
MARVEL
25 .com
CAPTAIN AMERICA
Steve Rogers, aka Captain America, led the forces opposed to the Registration Act
DEATH OF THE DREAM
DIRECT EDITION
RATED T+
$3.99 US $4.75 CAN

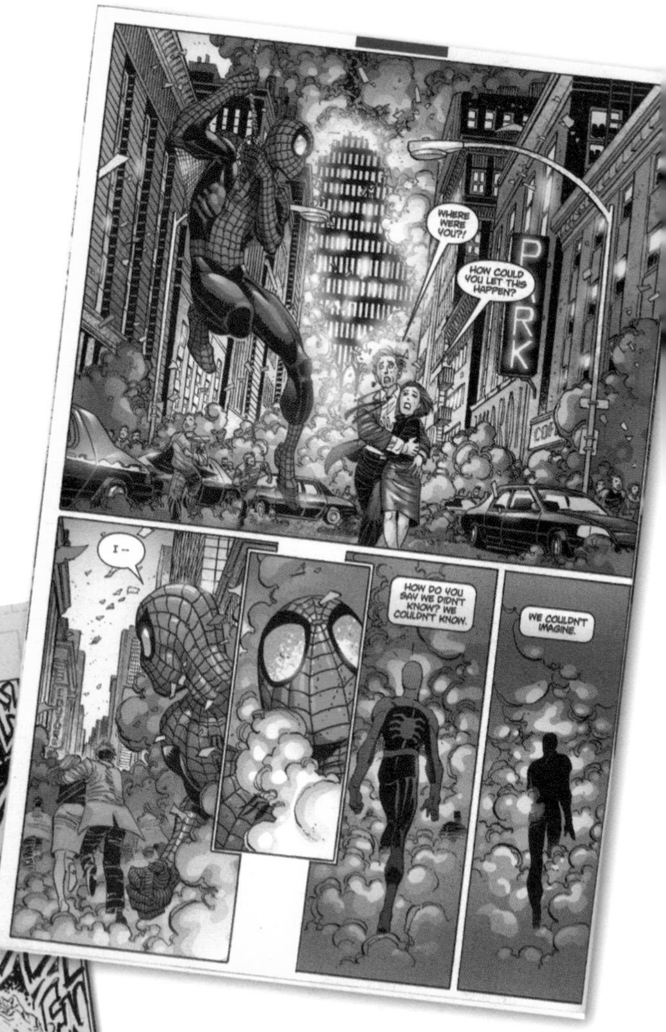
WHERE WERE YOU?!
HOW COULD YOU LET THIS HAPPEN?
PARK
I --
HOW DO YOU SAY WE DIDN'T KNOW? WE COULDN'T KNOW.
WE COULDN'T IMAGINE.

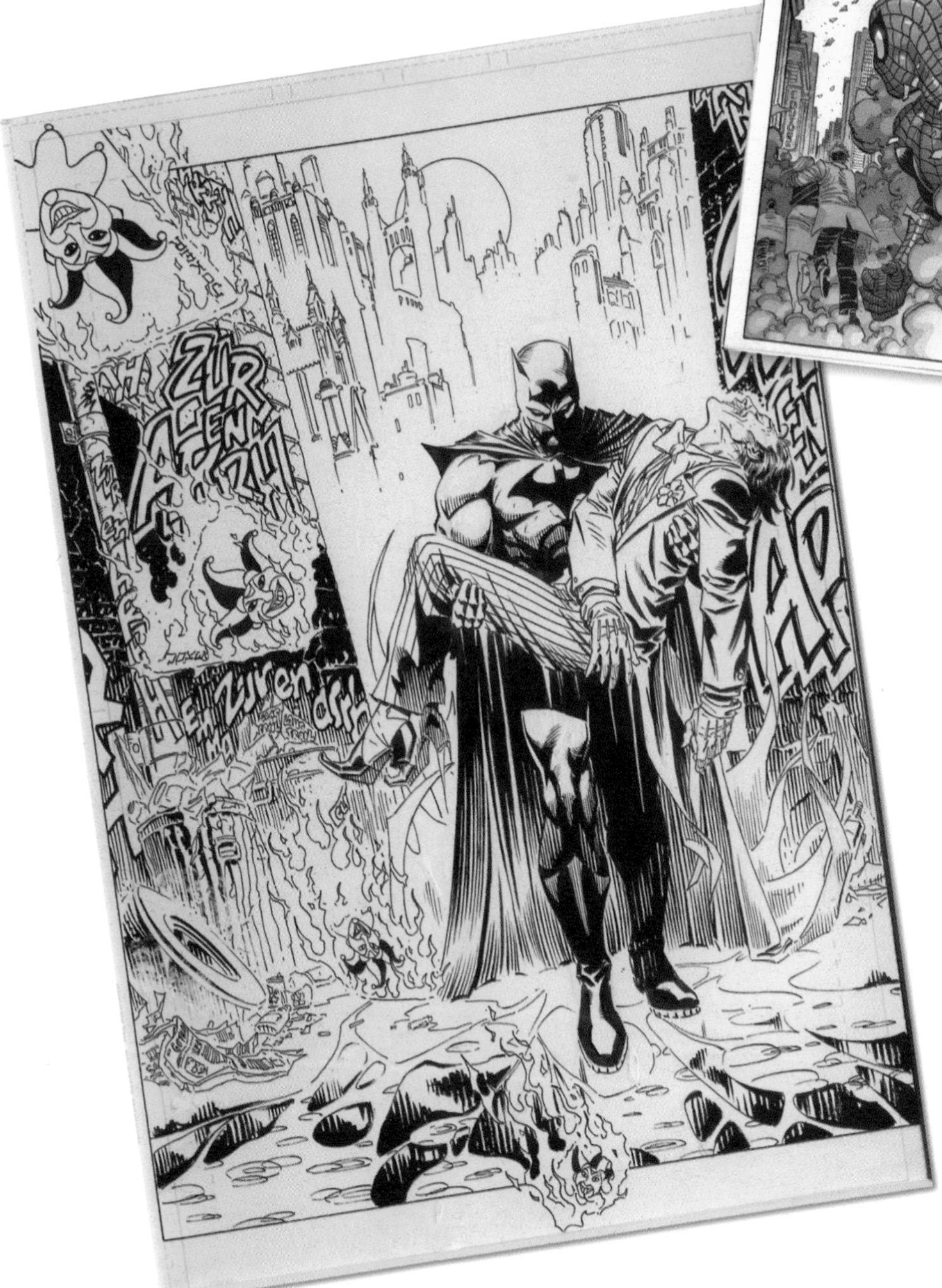

JOHN ROMITA, JR., penciller and SCOTT HANNA, inker
Interior page of THE AMAZING SPIDER-MAN Vol. 2 #36 (Marvel Comics, December 2001)
Collection of Rich Sheinaus

ANDY KUBERT
Original art for interior page of BATMAN #655 (DC Comics, September 2006)
Collection of Andy Kubert
(included in the exhibition *Comic Book Legends: Joe, Adam and Andy Kubert* at the Montclair Art Museum.)

AT RIGHT:

SCOT EATON, penciller and KLAUS JANSON, inker
Interior page of BLACK PANTHER, Vol. 3 #12 (Marvel Comics, March 2006)
Private Collection

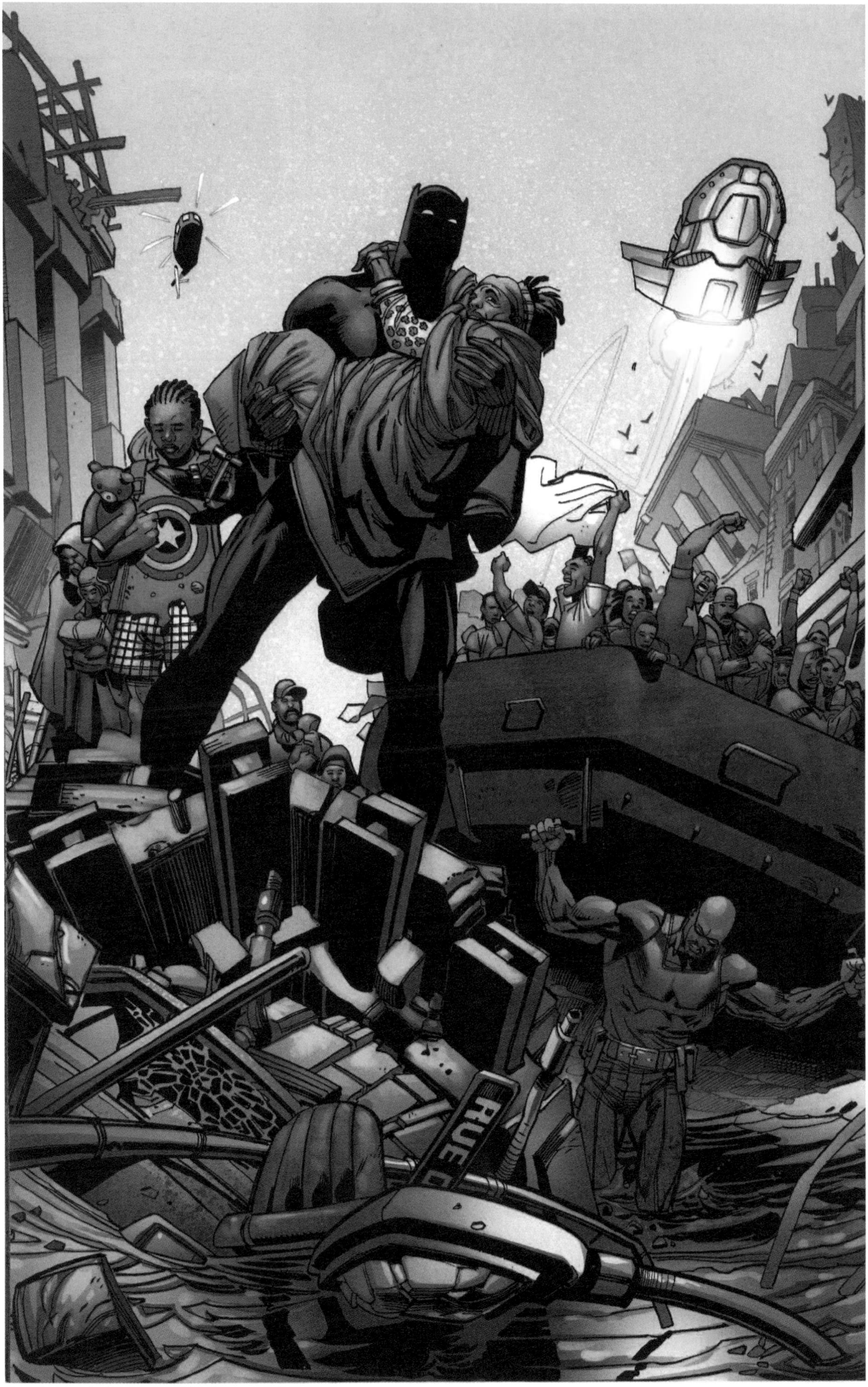
RUE

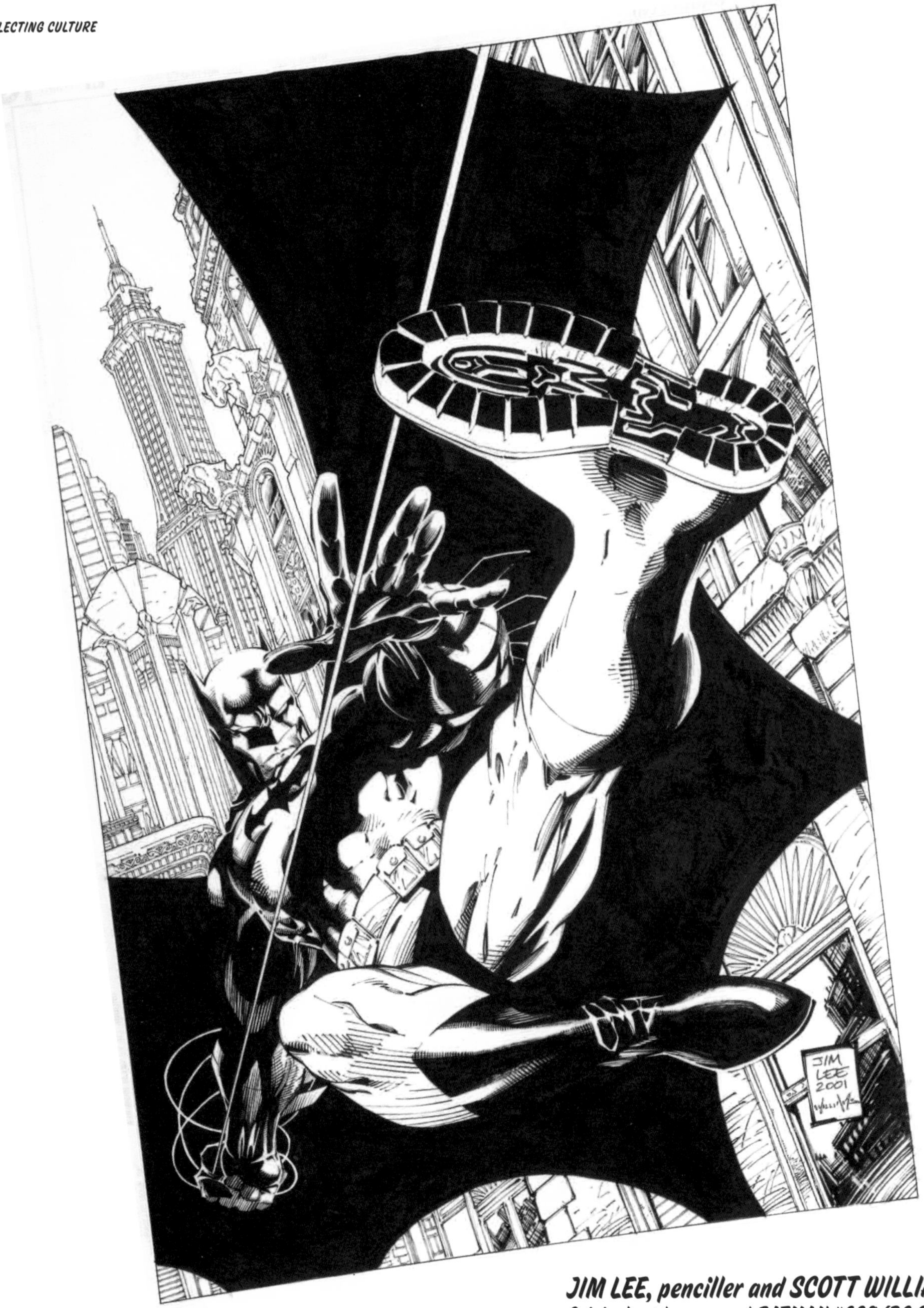
JIM LEE 2001

JIM LEE, penciller and SCOTT WILLIAMS, inker
Original art for cover of BATMAN #608 (DC Comics, December 2002)
Pen and ink on paper
Collection of Scott Williams

AT RIGHT:

ADAM HUGHES
Original art for the cover of WONDER WOMAN: THE ULTIMATE GUIDE TO THE AMAZON PRINCESS (Dorling Kindersley, 2003)
Pen and ink on paper
Collection of Steven Lee

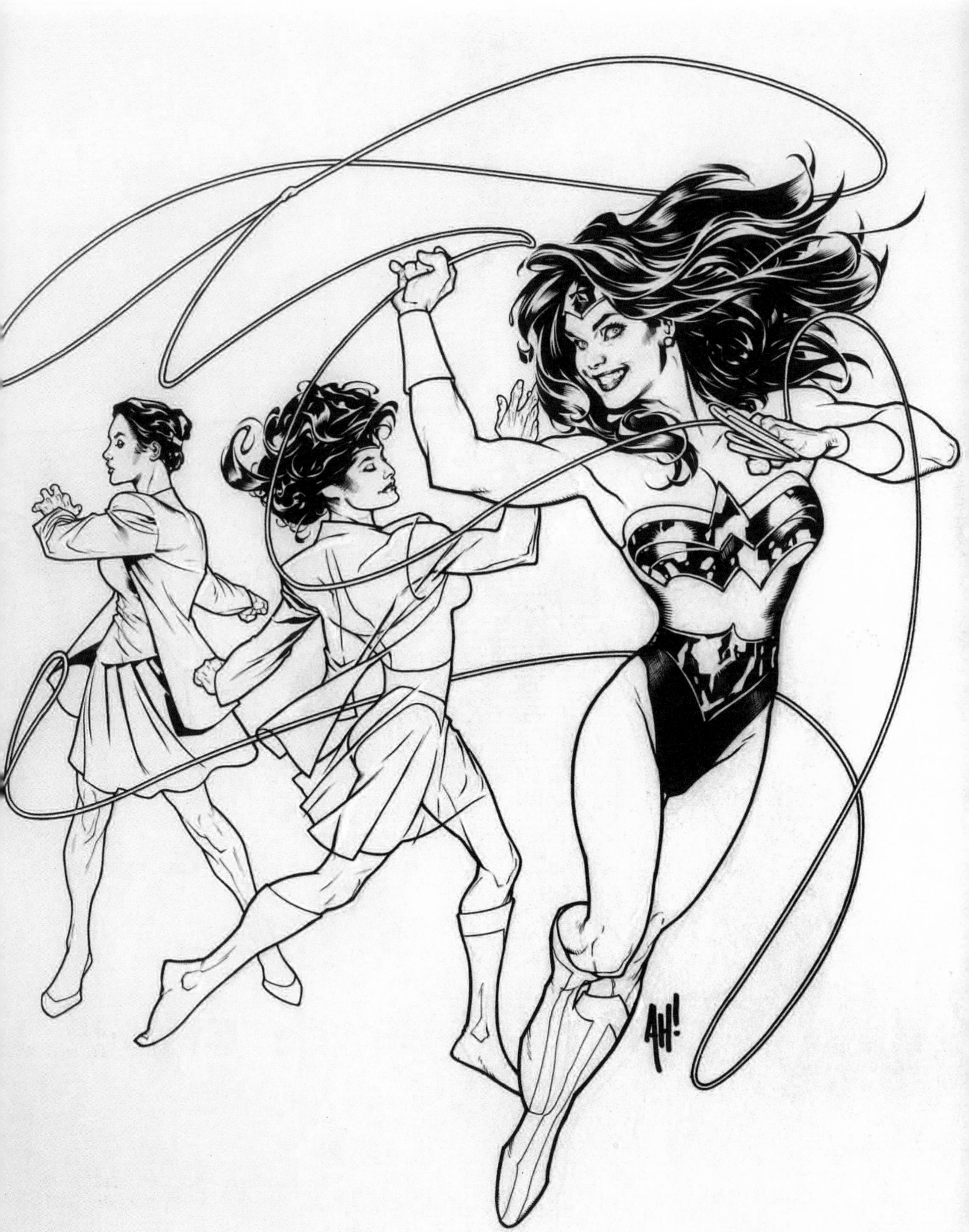
AH!

EXHIBITION CHECKLIST

SECTION I.   SUPER HEROES GO TO WAR: THE DEPRESSION & NEW DEAL 1938-1945

COMIC BOOKS

1. JOE SHUSTER (cover artist), JERRY SIEGEL, writer
ACTION COMICS #1 (DC Comics, June 1938)
Collection of Win Murray

2. BOB KANE, cover artist
DETECTIVE COMICS #27 (DC Comics, May 1939)
Collection of Eric Roberts

3. (Attributed to) JOE SHUSTER, cover artist
SUPERMAN #4 (DC Comics, Spring 1940)
Courtesy of MetropolisComics.com

4. (Attributed to) JOE SHUSTER, cover artist
SUPERMAN #5 (DC Comics, September/October 1940)
Collection of Ankur and Indu Jetley

5. JACK BURNLEY, cover artist
ACTION COMICS #59 (DC Comics, April 1943)
Collection of Ankur and Indu Jetley

6. FRED RAY, cover artist
SUPERMAN #17 (DC Comics, July/August 1942)
Collection of Ankur and Indu Jetley

7. BOB KANE, cover penciller and JERRY ROBINSON, cover inker
DETECTIVE COMICS #43 (DC Comics, September 1940)
Courtesy of MetropolisComics.com

8. JACK BURNLEY, JERRY ROBINSON, and possibly VINCE SULLIVAN (background), cover artists
NEW YORK WORLD'S FAIR COMICS (DC Comics, 1940)
Collection of Joseph P. Latino

9. JERRY ROBINSON, cover artist
BATMAN #17 (DC Comics, June/July 1943)
Courtesy of MetropolisComics.com

10. JACK BURNLEY, cover artist
WORLD'S FINEST COMICS #9 (DC Comics, Spring 1943)
Courtesy of MetropolisComics.com

11. JACK BURNLEY, cover artist
WORLD'S FINEST COMICS #11 (DC Comics, Fall 1943)
Courtesy of MetropolisComics.com

12. JACK KIRBY, cover penciller and JOE SIMON, cover inker
CAPTAIN AMERICA COMICS #1 (Marvel Comics, March 1941)
Collection of Jon Berk

13. JACK KIRBY, cover penciller and JOE SIMON, cover inker
CAPTAIN AMERICA COMICS #2 (Marvel Comics, April 1941)
Collection of Jon Berk

14. JACK KIRBY, cover penciller and JOE SIMON, cover inker
CAPTAIN AMERICA COMICS #8 (Marvel Comics, November 1941)
Collection of Jon Berk

15. C. C. BECK, cover artist
WHIZ COMICS #24 (Fawcett Publications, November 1941)
Collection of P.C. Hamerlinck

16. C. C. BECK, cover artist
CAPTAIN MARVEL ADVENTURES #8 (Fawcett Publications, March 1942)
Collection of Maggie Thompson

17. C. C. BECK, cover artist
CAPTAIN MARVEL ADVENTURES #21 (Fawcett Publications, February 12, 1943)
Courtesy of MetropolisComics.com

18. IRWIN HASEN, cover artist
GREEN LANTERN #4 (DC Comics, July 1942)
Collection of Steve Carey

19. HARRY G. PETER, cover artist
SENSATION COMICS #1 (DC Comics, January 1942)
Collection of Ankur and Indu Jetley

20. HARRY G. PETER, cover artist
WONDER WOMAN #1 (DC Comics, Summer 1942)
Collection of Michigan State University Libraries

21. HARRY G. PETER, cover artist
SENSATION COMICS #8 (DC Comics, August 1942)
Courtesy of Heritage Auction Galleries

22. HARRY G. PETER, cover artist
SENSATION COMICS #13 (DC Comics, January 1943)
Courtesy of Heritage Auction Galleries

23. EVERETT E. HIBBARD, cover artist
ALL STAR COMICS #4 (DC Comics, March-April 1941)
Courtesy of MetropolisComics.com

24. JOE GALLAGHER, cover artist
ALL STAR COMICS #24 (DC Comics, Spring 1945)
Courtesy of Heritage Auction Galleries

ORIGINAL COMIC ART

25. WINSOR MCCAY
LITTLE NEMO IN SLUMBERLAND
Original newspaper page from *The Sunday Record-Herald*
May 20, 1906
Collection of Joseph Veteri

26. HARRY G. PETER
WONDER WOMAN, 1940s
Original artwork for comic strip
Pen and ink on paper
Collection of Michael Uslan

27. JACK BURNLEY
Original artwork for *SUPERMAN SUNDAY COMIC STRIP,* September 5, 1943
Pencil and ink on paper
Collection of Daniel and Louise Herman

28. FRED RAY
Original art for the cover of *ACTION COMICS* #50 (DC Comics, July 1942)
Pen and ink on paper
Collection of Joe and Nadia Mannarino

29. GEORGE TUSKA
Original art for interior page of *CAPTAIN MARVEL* #4 (Fawcett Publications, October 1941)
Pen and ink on paper
Collection of Michael Uslan

30. JERRY ROBINSON
Original art for cover of *DETECTIVE COMICS* #60 (DC Comics, February 1942)
Pen, ink, and pencil on paper
Courtesy of Stephen Fishler, President of MetropolisComics.com

31. HARRY G. PETER
Original art for *WONDER WOMAN* unpublished splash page, *"RACKETEER'S BAIT!"* 1940s
Pen and ink on paper
Courtesy of Stephen Fishler, President of MetropolisComics.com

32. JOE SIMON
Original art for unpublished cover of *CAPTAIN AMERICA* #7 (Marvel Comics, October 1941)
Pen and ink on paper
Collection of Joe and Nadia Mannarino

33. JOE SIMON and JACK KIRBY/SIMON AND KIRBY PRODUCTIONS
CAPTAIN AMERICA MODEL SHEET, 1941
Watercolor on paper
Collection of Joe and Nadia Mannarino

SECTION II.   COLD WAR, CONFORMITY & CENSORSHIP: SUPER HEROES IN THE POSTWAR ERA & 1950s

COMIC BOOKS & OTHER PUBLICATIONS

34. DR. FREDERIC WERTHAM
SEDUCTION OF THE INNOCENT (New York: Holt, Rinehart, and Winston, 1954)
Collection of Michael Uslan

ROMANCE & AMERICANA

35. JACK BURNLEY, cover penciller and GEORGE ROUSSOS, cover inker
SUPERMAN #38 (DC Comics, January/February 1946)
Collection of Ankur and Indu Jetley

36. MARTIN NAYDEL, cover artist
ALL-FLASH #25 (DC Comics, October/November 1946)
Collection of Joseph P. Latino

37. JACK BURNLEY, cover penciller and CHARLES PARIS, cover inker
WORLD'S FINEST COMICS #26 (DC Comics, January/February 1947)
Collection of Paul Leggett

38. CURT SWAN, cover penciller and STAN KAYE, cover inker
SUPERBOY #57 (DC Comics, June 1957)
Private Collection

SECTION II.   COLD WAR, CONFORMITY & CENSORSHIP *Continued*

39. AL PLASTINO, cover penciller and STAN KAYE, cover inker
SUPERMAN #67 (DC Comics, November/December 1950)
Courtesy of MetropolisComics.com

40. IRWIN HASEN, cover artist
SENSATION COMICS #97 (DC Comics, May/June 1950)
Courtesy of Heritage Auction Galleries

41. J. WINSLOW MORTIMER, cover artist
SUPERBOY #34 (DC Comics, July 1954)
Collection of Rich Sheinaus

42. CURT SWAN, cover penciller and STAN KAYE, cover inker
SUPERBOY #36 (DC Comics, November 1954)
Courtesy of MetropolisComics.com

IMAGES OF SUPER HEROES & NATIVE AMERICAN CULTURE IN COMIC BOOKS OF THE POSTWAR ERA

43. JOE KUBERT, cover artist
FLASH COMICS #94 (DC Comics, April 1948)
Collection of Dan Makara

44. C.C. BECK, cover artist
CAPTAIN MARVEL ADVENTURES #83 (Fawcett Publications, April 1948)
Collection of Ankur and Indu Jetley

45. J. WINSLOW MORTIMER, cover artist
WORLD'S FINEST COMICS #58 (DC Comics, May/June 1952)
Collection of Alan Bartholomew

46. DICK SPRANG, cover penciller and CHARLES PARIS, cover inker
BATMAN #66 (DC Comics, August/September 1951)
Courtesy of MetropolisComics.com

47. J. WINSLOW MORTIMER, cover artist
BATMAN #86 (DC Comics, September 1955)
Collection of Paul Leggett

COMMUNISM, CONFORMITY, ATOMIC FEARS & SCIENCE FICTION

48. WAYNE BORING, cover penciller and STAN KAYE, cover inker
ACTION COMICS #101 (DC Comics, October 1946)
Collection of Dan Cusimano

49. C.C. BECK, cover artist
CAPTAIN MARVEL ADVENTURES #66 (Fawcett Publications, October 1946)
Courtesy of MetropolisComics.com

50. MARTIN NAYDEL, cover artist
ALL-FLASH #28 (DC Comics, April/May 1947)
Courtesy of MetropolisComics.com

51. C.C. BECK, artist
Interior pages of *CAPTAIN MARVEL ADVENTURES* #113 (Fawcett Publications, October 1950)
Private Collection

52. WAYNE BORING, cover penciller and STAN KAYE, cover inker
SUPERMAN #62 (DC Comics, January/February 1950)
Courtesy of MetropolisComics.com

53. JOHN ROMITA, SR., cover artist
CAPTAIN AMERICA COMICS #78 (Marvel Comics, September 1954)
Collection of Alan Bartholomew

54. CARMINE INFANTINO, cover penciller and JOE KUBERT, cover inker
SHOWCASE #4 (DC Comics, September-October 1956)
Collection of Michael Uslan

55. ROSS ANDRU, cover penciller and MIKE ESPOSITO, cover inker
WONDER WOMAN #95 (DC Comics, January 1958)
Collection of Alan Bartholomew

56. ROSS ANDRU, cover penciller and MIKE ESPOSITO, cover inker
WONDER WOMAN #99 (DC Comics, July 1958)
Collection of Alan Bartholomew

ORIGINAL COMIC ART

57. J. WINSLOW MORTIMER
Original art for cover of *WORLD'S FINEST COMICS* #33 (DC Comics, March/April 1948)
Pen and ink on paper
Courtesy of Stephen Fishler, President of MetropolisComics.com

58. IRWIN HASEN, penciller and BERNARD SACHS, inker
Original art for cover of *SENSATION COMICS* #96 (DC Comics, March/April 1950)
Pencil and ink on paper
Courtesy of Stephen Fishler, President of MetropolisComics.com

59. CURT SWAN, penciller and STAN KAYE, inker
Original art for interior page of *WORLD'S FINEST COMICS* #74 (DC Comics, January-February 1955)
Pen and ink on paper
Courtesy of Stephen Fishler, President of MetropolisComics.com

60. PAUL REINMAN
Original art for interior page of *ALL-AMERICAN COMICS* #89 (DC Comics, September 1947)
Pen and ink on paper
Collection of Ethan Roberts

61. LEOPOLD "LEE" ELIAS
Original art for cover of *ALL-FLASH* #30 (DC Comics, August/September 1947)
Pen and ink on paper
Collection of Joseph P. Latino

62. DICK SPRANG, penciller and CHARLES PARIS, inker
Original art for splash page of *BATMAN* #57 (February/March 1950)
Pen and ink on paper
Collection of Daniel and Louise Herman

63. WILL EISNER
Original drawing for unknown newspaper page 7 of *THE SPIRIT SECTION*, May 23, 1948
Pen and ink on paper
Collection of Ethan Roberts

SECTION III.   QUESTIONING AUTHORITY: SUPER HEROES & SOCIOPOLITICAL CHANGE IN THE 1960s & 70s

THE HUMANIZATION OF SUPER HEROES AS FALLIBLE INDIVIDUALS IN THE 60s & 70s

64. JACK KIRBY, cover penciller and DICK AYERS, cover inker
THE FANTASTIC FOUR #7 (Marvel Comics, October 1962)
Courtesy of MetropolisComics.com

65. JACK KIRBY, cover penciller and DICK AYERS, cover inker
THE FANTASTIC FOUR #9 (Marvel Comics, December 1962)
Courtesy of MetropolisComics.com

66. JACK KIRBY, cover penciller, and STEVE DITKO, cover inker
AMAZING FANTASY #15 (Marvel Comics, August 1962)
Collection of Michael Uslan

67. STEVE DITKO, artist
Interior page of *THE AMAZING SPIDER-MAN* #4 (Marvel Comics, September 1963)
Collection of Michael Uslan

68. JOHN ROMITA, SR., cover penciller
THE AMAZING SPIDER-MAN #50 (Marvel Comics, July 1967)
Collection of Joseph P. Latino

69. CARMINE INFANTINO, cover artist
ACTION COMICS #368 (DC Comics, October 1965)
Private Collection

70. NEAL ADAMS, cover artist
SUPERMAN #240 (DC Comics, July 1971)
Private Collection

THE SUPER HERO/ANTI-HERO OF THE COUNTERCULTURE GENERATION: QUESTIONING AUTHORITY

71. GENE COLAN, penciller and JOE SINNOTT, inker
Interior page of *CAPTAIN AMERICA* #122 (Marvel Comics, February 1970)
Collection of Scott Webb

72. JOHN ROMITA, SR., cover artist
THE AMAZING SPIDER-MAN #68 (Marvel Comics, January 1969)
Courtesy of MetropolisComics.com

SECTION III. QUESTIONING AUTHORITY *Continued*

73. GENE COLAN, cover penciller and JOE SINNOTT, cover inker
CAPTAIN AMERICA #120
(Marvel Comics, December 1969)
Collection of Michigan State University Libraries

74. NEAL ADAMS, cover penciller and DICK GIORDANO, cover inker
ACTION COMICS #398 (DC Comics, March 1971)
Collection of Rich Sheinaus

75. GIL KANE, cover penciller and FRANK GIACOIA, cover inker
THE AMAZING SPIDER-MAN #99 (Marvel Comics, August 1971)
Courtesy of MetropolisComics.com

SUPER HEROES AND POPULAR CULTURE IN THE 1960s & 70s

76. CURT SWAN, cover penciller and GEORGE KLEIN, cover inker
ACTION COMICS #345 (DC Comics, January 1967)
Private Collection

77. CURT SWAN, cover penciller and GEORGE KLEIN, cover inker
SUPERMAN'S PAL JIMMY OLSEN #79 (DC Comics, September 1964)
Collection of Michael Uslan

78. JACK KIRBY, cover penciller and CHIC STONE, cover inker
STRANGE TALES #130 (Marvel Comics, March 1964)
Collection of Michael Uslan

79. CARMINE INFANTINO, cover penciller and MURPHY ANDERSON, cover inker
BATMAN #183 (DC Comics, August 1966)
Private Collection

80. MIKE SEKOWSKY, cover penciller and DICK GIORDANO, cover inker
WONDER WOMAN #178 (DC Comics, September-October 1968)
Collection of Rich Sheinaus

81. NEAL ADAMS, cover penciller and DICK GIORDANO, cover inker
BATMAN #222 (DC Comics, June 1970)
Collection of Rich Sheinaus

82. NEAL ADAMS, cover artist
All New Collectors' Edition, SUPERMAN VS. MUHAMMAD ALI
(DC Comics, Inc., 1978)
Collection of Michael Uslan

83. DAVE COCKRUM, cover penciller and MARIE SEVERIN, cover inker
MARVEL TEAM-UP #74
(Marvel Comics, October 1978)
Private Collection

SUPER HEROES AND POLITICAL FIGURES IN THE 1960s

84. AL PLASTINO, artist
Interior page for *SUPERMAN* #170
(DC Comics, July 1964)
Private Collection

85. JIM MOONEY, artist
Interior page for *ACTION COMICS* #285
(DC Comics, February 1962)
Collection of Michael Uslan

SUPER HEROES AND FEMINISM IN THE 1960s & 70s

86. NEAL ADAMS, cover penciller and NICK CARDY, cover inker
DC SPECIAL No. 3, All-Girl Issue (DC Comics, April/June 1969)
Courtesy of MetropolisComics.com

87. NEAL ADAMS, cover artist
BATMAN #210 (DC Comics, March 1969)
Collection of Rich Sheinaus

88. JOHN BUSCEMA, cover artist
THE AVENGERS #83 (Marvel Comics, December 1970)
Collection of Scott Webb

89. MURPHY ANDERSON, cover artist
Cover illustration for *MS. MAGAZINE* No. 1 (July 1972)
Private Collection

90. DICK GIORDANO, cover artist
WONDER WOMAN #203
(DC Comics, December 1972)
Collection of Michigan State University Libraries

SUPER HEROES AND ECOLOGY DURING THE 1960s & 70s

91. NEAL ADAMS, cover artist
JUSTICE LEAGUE OF AMERICA #79 (DC Comics, March 1970)
Collection of Michael Uslan

92. JOHN BUSCEMA, cover penciller and JOE SINNOTT, cover inker
THE SILVER SURFER #1 (Marvel Comics, August 1968)
Collection of Michael Uslan

SUPER HEROES, THE VIET NAM WAR, AND WATERGATE

93. JOE KUBERT, cover artist
SUPERMAN #216 (DC Comics, May 1969)
Private Collection

94. JACK KIRBY, cover penciller and CHIC STONE, cover inker
TALES OF SUSPENSE #61
(Marvel Comics, January 1965)
Courtesy of MetropolisComics.com

95. JOHN ROMITA, SR., cover artist
CAPTAIN AMERICA #176 (Marvel Comics, August 1974)
Collection of Michigan State University Libraries

SUPER HEROES AND ANTI-DRUG MESSAGES: SPIDER-MAN, GREEN LANTERN AND GREEN ARROW

96. GIL KANE, cover artist
THE AMAZING SPIDER-MAN #96
(Marvel Comics, May 1971)
Courtesy of MetropolisComics.com

97. NEAL ADAMS, cover artist
GREEN LANTERN/GREEN ARROW #85
(DC Comics, August/September 1971)
Collection of Michael Uslan

SUPER HEROES, MULTICULTURAL DIVERSITY, AND RACIAL TOLERANCE IN THE 1960s & 70s

98. JACK KIRBY, cover artist
THE X-MEN #1 (Marvel Comics, September 1963)
Collection of Michael Uslan

99. DON HECK, cover art
THE AVENGERS #33 (Marvel Comics, October 1965)
Courtesy of MetropolisComics.com

100. JACK KIRBY, cover penciller and JOE SINNOTT, inker
FANTASTIC FOUR #52 (Marvel Comics, July 1966)
Collection of Michael Uslan

101. CARMINE INFANTINO, cover penciller and MURPHY ANDERSON, cover inker
JUSTICE LEAGUE OF AMERICA #57 (DC Comics, November 1967)
Collection of Michael Uslan

102. JACK KIRBY, cover artist
CAPTAIN AMERICA #117
(Marvel Comics, September 1969)
Collection of Scott Webb

103. NEAL ADAMS, cover artist
Interior page of *GREEN LANTERN/GREEN ARROW* #76 (DC Comics, April 1970)
Collection of Michael Uslan

104. NEAL ADAMS, cover artist
GREEN LANTERN/GREEN ARROW #79 (DC Comics, September 1970)
Collection of Michael Uslan

105. CURT SWAN, cover penciller and MURPHY ANDERSON, cover inker
ACTION COMICS #401 (DC Comics, June 1971)
Collection of Le Brun Library, Montclair Art Museum

106. NEAL ADAMS, cover artist
GREEN LANTERN/GREEN ARROW #87 (DC Comics, December 1971/January 1972)
Collection of Michael Uslan

107. JOHN ROMITA, SR., cover artist
LUKE CAGE, HERO FOR HIRE #1 (Marvel Comics, June 1972)
Collection of Michael Uslan

108. JAMES STARLIN, cover penciller and AL MILGROM, cover inker
SPECIAL MARVEL EDITION #15 (Marvel Comics, December 1973)
Collection of Scott Webb

109. DAVE COCKRUM, cover artist
GIANT SIZE X-MEN # 1 (Marvel Comics, Summer 1975)
Collection of Michael Uslan

110. JOHN ROMITA, SR., cover artist
JUNGLE ACTION #21
(Marvel Comics, May 1976)
Private Collection

ORIGINAL COMIC ART

111. JOE KUBERT
Stats/color separations for *OUR ARMY AT WAR* #196 (DC Comics, August 1968)
Collection of Joe and Nadia Mannarino

SECTION III.   QUESTIONING AUTHORITY *Continued*

112. STEVE DITKO
Original art for interior page of *THE AMAZING SPIDER-MAN* #10 (Marvel Comics, March 1964)
Pen and ink on paper
Collection of Michael Uslan

113. CURT SWAN, penciller and GEORGE KLEIN, inker
Original art for cover of *ACTION COMICS* #357 (DC Comics, December 1967)
Pen and ink on paper
Courtesy of Stephen Fishler, President of MetropolisComics.com

114. CARMINE INFANTINO, penciller and JOE GIELLA, inker
Original art for cover of *DETECTIVE COMICS* #327 (DC Comics, May 1964)
Pen and ink on paper
Courtesy of Stephen Fishler, President of MetropolisComics.com

115. CARMINE INFANTINO, penciller and JOE GIELLA, inker
Original art for interior page of *THE FLASH* #135 (DC Comics, March 1963)
Pen and ink on paper
Collection of Daniel and Louise Herman

116. CARMINE INFANTINO, penciller and MURPHY ANDERSON, inker
Original art for cover of *JUSTICE LEAGUE OF AMERICA* #57 (DC Comics, November 1967)
Pen and ink on paper
Courtesy of Stephen Fishler, President of MetropolisComics.com

117. GIL KANE, penciller and MURPHY ANDERSON, inker
Original art for the cover of *GREEN LANTERN* #26, (DC Comics, January 1964)
Pen and ink on paper
Collection of Daniel and Louise Herman

118. MIKE SEKOWSKY, penciller and JOE GIELLA, inker
Original art for cover of *GREEN LANTERN* #65 (DC Comics, December 1968)
Pen and ink on paper
Courtesy of Stephen Fishler, President of MetropolisComics.com

119. CURT SWAN, penciller and MURPHY ANDERSON, inker
Original art for the cover of *ACTION COMICS* #380, (DC Comics, September 1969)
Pen and ink on paper
Collection of Daniel and Louise Herman

120. IRV NOVICK
Original art for the cover of *WONDER WOMAN* #174 (DC Comics, January/February 1968)
Pen and ink on paper
Collection of Daniel and Louise Herman

121. STEVE DITKO
Original art for splash page of *THE AMAZING SPIDER-MAN* #8 (Marvel Comics, January 1964)
Pen and ink on paper
Collection of Joe and Nadia Mannarino

122. JACK KIRBY, penciller and JOE SINNOTT, inker
Original art for interior page of *THE FANTASTIC FOUR* #5 (Marvel Comics, July 1962)
Pen and ink on paper
Collection of Joe and Nadia Mannarino

123. NEAL ADAMS
Original art for the cover of *THE BRAVE AND THE BOLD* #88 (DC Comics, March 1970)
Pen and ink on paper
Collection of Joe and Nadia Mannarino

124. DAVE COCKRUM
Original art for the cover of *THE X-MEN* #105 (Marvel Comics, June 1977)
Pen and ink on paper
Collection of Joe and Nadia Mannarino

125. JOHN ROMITA, SR.
Original art for the cover of *THE AMAZING SPIDER-MAN* #75 (Marvel Comics, August 1969)
Pen and ink on paper
Collection of Srihari S. Naidu, M.D.

126. JOHN BUSCEMA
Original art for the splash page of *THE SILVER SURFER* #14 (Marvel Comics, March 1970)
Pen and ink on paper
Collection of Srihari S. Naidu, M.D.

127. NEAL ADAMS
Original art for the cover of *GREEN LANTERN/GREEN ARROW* #87 (DC Comics, December 1971/January 1972)
Ink on paper
Collection of Scott Williams

128. JACK KIRBY
Original art for interior page of *MARVEL TREASURY SPECIAL...FEATURING CAPTAIN AMERICA'S BICENTENNIAL BATTLES* (Marvel Comics, 1976)
Pen and ink on paper
Collection of Michael Uslan

129. JOE KUBERT
Original art for the cover of *BATMAN* #310 (DC Comics, April 1979)
Pen and ink on paper
Collection of Joe Kubert

130. GENE COLAN
Original art for interior page of *CAPTAIN AMERICA* #126 (DC Comics, June 1970)
Pen and ink on paper
Collection of Srihari S. Naidu, M.D.

131. NEAL ADAMS
Original art for interior page of *DETECTIVE COMICS* #408 (DC Comics, February 1971)
Pen and ink on paper
Collection of Srihari S. Naidu, M.D.

SECTION IV.   AMERICAN INDIAN SUPER HEROES: STEREOTYPES & REALITIES

132. JACK KIRBY, cover penciller and JOE SINNOTT, cover inker
MARVEL'S GREATEST COMICS #62 (Marvel Comics, March 1976)
Collection of Le Brun Library, Montclair Art Museum

133. BOB MCLEOD, cover penciller and MIKE GUSTOVICH, cover inker
THE NEW MUTANTS #3 (Marvel Comics, May 1983)
Collection of Le Brun Library, Montclair Art Museum

134. ERNIE COLON, cover penciller and DICK GIORDANO, cover inker
ARAK, SON OF THUNDER #1 (DC Comics, September 1981)
Collection of Le Brun Library, Montclair Art Museum

135. ERNIE COLON, cover penciller and DICK GIORDANO, cover inker
ARAK, SON OF THUNDER #2 (DC Comics, October 1981)
Collection of Le Brun Library, Montclair Art Museum

136. NEAL ADAMS, cover artist
MARVEL SPOTLIGHT #1 (Marvel Comics, November 1971)
Collection of Le Brun Library, Montclair Art Museum

137. JOHN BUSCEMA, cover penciller and TOM PALMER, cover inker
THE AVENGERS #80 (Marvel Comics, September 1970)
Collection of Le Brun Library, Montclair Art Museum

138. J. SCOTT CAMPBELL and ALEX GARNER, cover artists
GEN 13 #3 (Image Comics, published by Wildstorm Comics, July 1995)
Collection of Le Brun Library, Montclair Art Museum

139. JOHN BYRNE, cover penciller and TERRY AUSTIN, cover inker
ALPHA FLIGHT #1 (Marvel Comics, August 1983)
Collection of Le Brun Library, Montclair Art Museum

140. SHEA ANTON PENSA, cover artist
THE BUTCHER #1 (DC Comics, May 1990)
Collection of Le Brun Library, Montclair Art Museum

141. DANIEL ACUÑA, cover artist
UNCLE SAM AND THE FREEDOM FIGHTERS #3 (DC Comics, November 2006)
Collection of Le Brun Library, Montclair Art Museum

142. STEVEN KEEWATIN SANDERSON, cover artist and writer
DARKNESS CALLS, (The Healthy Aboriginal Network, November 2006)
Collection of Le Brun Library, Montclair Art Museum

143. STEVE PREMO, cover artist
A HERO'S VOICE (The Mille Lacs Band of Ojibwe: Educational Comic Book Series, 1996)
Collection of Le Brun Library, Montclair Art Museum

SECTION IV.   AMERICAN INDIAN SUPER HEROES *Continued*

144. DIMI MACHERAS, cover artist
STRONG MAN #1 (Association of Alaska School Boards, February 2007)
Collection of Le Brun Library, Montclair Art Museum

145. RON FATTORUSO, cover penciller and MIKE KELLEHER, cover inker
PEACE PARTY #1 (Blue Corn Comics, 1999)
Collection of Le Brun Library, Montclair Art Museum

146. RON FRENZ, cover penciller and JOE SINNOTT, cover inker
NFL SUPERPRO #6 (Marvel Comics, March, 1992)
Collection of Le Brun Library, Montclair Art Museum

147. JOCK, cover artist
SCALPED #1 (Vertigo Comics, an imprint of DC Comics, March 2007)
Collection of Le Brun Library, Montclair Art Museum

SECTION V.   DIVERSITY & MORAL COMPLEXITY: SUPER HEROES OF THE 1980s & 1990s

COMIC BOOKS

DEATHS, VULNERABILITIES & RESURRECTIONS OF SUPER HERO ICONS

148. RON FRENZ, cover penciller and KLAUS JANSON, cover inker
THE AMAZING SPIDER-MAN #252 (Marvel Comics, May 1984)
Collection of Rich Sheinaus

149. TODD MCFARLANE, cover artist
THE AMAZING SPIDER-MAN #300 (Marvel Comics, May 1988)
Private Collection

150. GEORGE PEREZ, cover artist
CRISIS ON INFINITE EARTHS #7
(DC Comics, October 1985)
Collection of Rich Sheinaus

151. CURT SWAN, cover penciller and MURPHY ANDERSON, cover inker
ACTION COMICS #583 (DC Comics, September 1986)
Private Collection

152. JERRY ORDWAY, cover artist
THE ADVENTURES OF SUPERMAN #424 (DC Comics, January 1987)
Private Collection

153. GEORGE PEREZ, cover artist
WONDER WOMAN (vol. 2) #1
(DC Comics, February 1987)
Private Collection

154. DAVID MAZZUCCHELLI, cover artist
BATMAN #405 (DC Comics, March 1987)
Private Collection

155. MIKE MIGNOLA, cover artist
BATMAN #428 (D.C. Comics, March 1987)
Private Collection

156. JIM LEE, cover penciller and SCOTT WILLIAMS, cover inker
X-MEN #1 (Marvel Comics, October 1991)
Private Collection

157. DAN JURGENS, cover penciller and BRETT BREEDING, cover inker
SUPERMAN #76 (DC Comics, February 1993)
Private Collection

158. JON BOGDANOVE, penciller and DENNIS JANKE, inker
Interior page of *SUPERMAN: THE MAN OF STEEL* #20
(DC Comics, February 1993)
Private Collection

159. KELLEY JONES, cover artist
BATMAN #497 (DC Comics, July 1993)
Private Collection

BATMAN: THE DARK KNIGHT RETURNS & WATCHMEN

160. FRANK MILLER, cover penciller and writer, KLAUS JANSON, cover inker
BATMAN: THE DARK KNIGHT RETURNS: BOOK ONE (DC Comics, 1986)
Collection of Rich Sheinaus

161. FRANK MILLER, cover penciller and writer, KLAUS JANSON, cover inker
BATMAN: THE DARK KNIGHT RETURNS: BOOK TWO (DC Comics, 1986)
Collection of Rich Sheinaus

162. DAVE GIBBONS, cover artist
WATCHMEN #1 (DC Comics, September 1986)
Collection of Rich Sheinaus

163. DAVE GIBBONS, cover artist
WATCHMEN #12 (DC Comics, October 1987)
Collection of Rich Sheinaus

SUPER HEROES, SOCIAL ISSUES, POPULAR CULTURE, & MULTI-CULTURAL DIVERSITY: MILESTONE COMICS & OTHER VENTURES

164. GENE COLAN, cover penciller and ROMEO TANGHAL, cover inker
WONDER WOMAN #288 (DC Comics, February 1982)
Private Collection

165. AL MILGROM, cover penciller and JOE SINNOTT, cover inker
THE AVENGERS #239 (Marvel Comics, January 1984)
Collection of Scott Webb

166. ARTHUR ADAMS, cover artist
HEROES FOR HOPE STARRING THE X-MEN #1 (Marvel Comics, December 1985)
Private Collection

167. NEAL ADAMS and DICK GIORDANO, cover artists
HEROES AGAINST HUNGER #1 (DC Comics, 1986)
Private Collection

168. DAVE DORMAN, cover artist
BATMAN - SEDUCTION OF THE GUN #1
(DC Comics, February 1993)
Private Collection

169. DENYS COWAN, cover penciller and JIMMY PALMIOTTI, cover inker
HARDWARE #1 (Milestone, a division of DC Comics, April 1993)
Private Collection

170. DENYS COWAN, cover penciller and M.D. BRIGHT
ICON #1 (Milestone, a division of DC Comics, May 1993)
Private Collection

171. DENYS COWAN, cover penciller and JIMMY PALMIOTTI, cover inker
STATIC #1 (Milestone, a division of DC Comics, June 1993)
Collection of Rich Sheinaus

172. JOE STATON, cover penciller and BILL SIENKIEWICZ, cover inker
BATMAN: DEATH OF INNOCENTS #1 (DC Comics, December 1996)
Private Collection

173. TODD MCFARLANE, artist
SPIDER-MAN PLATINUM EDITION #1
(Marvel Comics, 1991)
Stats/color separations demonstrating the four-color process
Collection of Ankur and Indu Jetley

ORIGINAL COMIC ART

174. BRIAN BOLLAND
Original art for interior page of *BATMAN: THE KILLING JOKE* (DC Comics, 1988)
Pen and ink on paper
Collection of Srihari S. Naidu, M.D.

175. DAVE COCKRUM
Original art for splash page for *THE UNCANNY X-MEN* #147 (Marvel Comics, July 1981)
Pen and ink on paper
Collection of Srihari S. Naidu, M.D

176. DAVE GIBBONS
Original art for double page spread in *WATCHMEN* #12 (DC Comics, October 1987)
Pen and ink on paper
Collection of Srihari S. Naidu, M.D

177. JOE KUBERT
Original art for cover of
THE GREATEST HEROES OF THE 1950s
(DC Comics, 1990)
Watercolor on paper
Collection of Joe Kubert

SECTION V.   DIVERSITY & MORAL COMPLEXITY *Continued*

178. DAN JURGENS, penciller and BRETT BREEDING, inker
Original art for cover of *SUPERMAN* #76 (DC Comics, February 1993)
Pen and ink on paper
Collection of Srihari S. Naidu, M.D

179. FRANK MILLER
Original art for interior page of *BATMAN: THE DARK KNIGHT RETURNS: BOOK THREE,* (DC Comics, 1986)
Pen and ink on paper
Collection of Srihari S. Naidu, M.D

180. GENE COLAN
Original art for interior page of *WONDER WOMAN* #288 (DC Comics, February 1982)
Pen and ink on paper
Courtesy of Ben Smith, GothamCityArt.com

181. JOE KUBERT
Original art for cover of *ALL STAR SQUADRON* #15 (DC Comics, August 1982)
Pen and ink on paper
Collection of Joe Kubert

182. ALEX ROSS
Original art related to the cover of *HISTORY OF THE DC UNIVERSE* (DC Comics, 1986), 2002
Mixed media on paper
Collection of Ankur and Indu Jetley

183. ALEX ROSS
SUPERMAN: PEACE ON EARTH, 2000
Watercolor on paper
Collection of Ankur and Indu Jetley

184. JOHN PAUL LEON
Original art for interior page of *STATIC* #5 (Milestone, a division of DC Comics, October 1993)
Collection of Ethan Roberts

185. DENYS COWAN, penciller and PRENTIS ROLLINS, inker
Original art for interior page of *STATIC* #14 (Milestone, a division of DC Comics, August 1994)
Pen and ink on paper
Collection of Denys Cowan

186. GREG and TIM HILDEBRANDT
CAPTAIN AMERICA, 1994
Acrylic on board
Collection of Michael Uslan

187. STUART IMMONEN, penciller and AND JOSE MARZAN, JR., inker
Original art for double-page spread of *ACTION COMICS* #747 (DC Comics, August 1998)
Pen and ink on paper
Collection of Rich Sheinaus

188. ANDY KUBERT, penciller and MATT RYAN, inker
Original art for *X-MEN* (second series) wrap-around cover #25 (Marvel Comics, October 1993)
Pen and ink on paper
Collection of Andy Kubert

189. ADAM KUBERT
Original art for interior page of *X-MEN* #81 (Marvel Comics, November 1998)
Ink and pencil on paper
Collection of Adam Kubert

190. GEORGES JEANTY, penciller and DOUG HAZLEWOOD, inker
Original art for interior page of *TEAM SUPERMAN* #1 (DC Comics, July 1999)
Pen and ink on paper
Collection of Ankur and Indu Jetley

SECTION VI.   SUPER HEROES AT GROUND ZERO: THE NEW CENTURY

191.
Black cover for THE AMAZING SPIDER-MAN Vol. 2, #36 (Marvel Comics, December 2001)
Collection of Rich Sheinaus

192. JOHN ROMITA, JR., penciller and SCOTT HANNA, inker
Interior page of *THE AMAZING SPIDER-MAN* Vol. 2, #36 (Marvel Comics, December 2001)
Collection of Rich Sheinaus

193. JOHN ROMITA, JR., cover artist
THE AMAZING SPIDER-MAN #508 (Marvel Comics, July 2004)
Collection of Rich Sheinaus

194. SAL VELLUTO with BOB ALMOND and CHRIS DICKEY; MIKE DEODATO, JR. with DENNIS CALERO
Interior pages of *HEROES* Vol. 1 No. 1 (Marvel Comics, second printing, December 2001)
Collection of Rich Sheinaus

195. ALEX ROSS, cover artist
THE WORLD'S FINEST COMIC BOOK WRITERS & ARTISTS TELL STORIES TO REMEMBER 9-11 SEPTEMBER 11TH 2001 (DC Comics, 2002)
Private Collection

196. TONY HARRIS, cover penciller and RAY SNYDER, cover inker
PRESIDENT LUTHOR SECRET FILES & ORIGINS #1 (DC Comics, March 2001)
Private Collection

197. LEONARD KIRK, cover penciller and ROBIN RIGGS, cover inker
SUPERGIRL #65 (February 2002)
Private Collection

198. CHRIS CROSS, penciller and TOM NGUYEN inker
Interior page of *JUSTICE LEAGUE OF AMERICA* #83 (DC Comics, September 2003)
Private Collection

199. MICHAEL USLAN, writer and PETER SNEJBJERG, artist
Interior pages of *BATMAN DETECTIVE NO. 27* (DC Comics, 2003)
Collection of Michael Uslan

200. J.G. JONES and ALEX SINCLAIR, cover artists
52 WEEK ELEVEN (DC Comics, July 19, 2006)
Private Collection

201. DUNCAN ROULEAU, cover artist
BLUE BEETLE #6 (DC Comics, October 2006)
Private Collection

202. SCOT EATON, penciller and KLAUS JANSON, inker
Interior page of *BLACK PANTHER*, vol. 3 #12 (Marvel Comics, March 2006)
Private Collection

203. STEVE MCNIVEN, penciller, DEXTER VINES, INKER; story by MARK MILLAR
CIVIL WAR #1 (Marvel Comics, July 2006)
Collection of Rich Sheinaus

204. STEVE MCNIVEN, penciller, DEXTER VINES, inker; story by MARK MILLAR
CIVIL WAR #2 (Marvel Comics, August 2006)
Private Collection

205. STEVE EPTING, cover artist
CAPTAIN AMERICA (CIVIL WAR EPILOGUE) #25 (Marvel Comics, April 2007)
Private Collection

ORIGINAL COMIC ART

206. ADAM HUGHES
Original art for the cover of Scott Beatty's *WONDER WOMAN: THE ULTIMATE GUIDE TO THE AMAZON PRINCESS* (Dorling Kindersley, 2003)
Pen and ink on paper
Collection of Steven Lee

207. JIM LEE, penciller and SCOTT WILLIAMS, inker
Original art for cover of *BATMAN* #608 (DC Comics, December 2002)
Pen and ink on paper
Collection of Scott Williams

208. SAL VELLUTO, penciller and MARK MCKENNA, inker
Original art for final splash page of *BLACK PANTHER* #29 (Marvel Comics, April 2001)
Pen and ink on paper
Courtesy of WildPig Comics II

209. GREG HILDEBRANDT
GOLDEN AND SILVER AGE MURAL SKETCHES, 2007
Pencil on paper
Courtesy of Spiderwebart.com

210. ADAM KUBERT
Original art for the cover of *ACTION COMICS* #844 (DC Comics, December 2006)
Ink and gouache on cardboard
Collection of Adam Kubert

211. STEVE MCNIVEN
Original art for interior pages of *CIVIL WAR* #2 (Marvel Comics, August 2006)
Pen and ink on Marvel Comics Bristol board
Collection of Steve McNiven

SECTION VI.   SUPER HEROES AT GROUND ZERO *Continued*

212. AMANDA CONNER
Original art for interior page of *SUPERGIRL* #12
(DC Comics, January 2007)
Pen and ink on paper
Collection of Amanda Conner

**213. ANDY KUBERT, penciller
and JOE KUBERT, inker**
Original art for the cover of *BATMAN* #664
(DC Comics, May 2007)
Pen and ink on paper
Collection of Andy Kubert

OTHER WORKS:

214. *BATMAN BEGINS*, 2005
Poster
Collection of Michael Uslan

215. *SUPERMAN*, c. 2004
Fiberglass statue
Generously donated by Mort and Patricia David for a
Raffle to benefit the Montclair Art Museum

216. *SPIDER-MAN*, 2003
Fiberglass statue
Collection of Ankur and Indu Jetley

BIBLIOGRAPHY
(ARRANGED CHRONOLOGICALLY)

Michael E. Uslan, *The Comic Book in America* (Indiana University Division of Continuing Education Independent Study Division, 1973).

Michael E. Uslan, *The Comic Book Revolution* (Indiana University School of Continuing Studies, Independent Study Division, 1977).

Michael E. Uslan, *America At War, The Best of DC War Comics* (New York: Simon and Shuster, 1979).

Mike Benton, *The Illustrated History of Superhero Comics of the Golden Age* (Dallas: Taylor Publishing Company, 1992).

Richard Reynolds, *Superheroes A Modern Mythology* (Jackson: University Press of Mississippi, 1992).

Scott McCloud, *Understanding Comics: The Invisible Art* (Northampton, Massachusetts: Tundra Publishing, 1993).

Joe Kubert, *Superheroes: Joe Kubert's Wonderful World of Comics* (Watson-Guptill Publishers, 1999)

Les Daniels, *Wonder Woman: The Life and Times of the Amazon Princess* (San Francisco: Chronicle Books, 2000).

Scott McCloud, *Reinventing Comics: How Imagination and Technology Are Revolutionizing an Art Form* (New York: HarperCollins Publishers, Inc., 2000).

Jeffrey A. Brown, *Black Superheroes, Milestone Comics, and Their Fans* (Jackson: University Press of Mississippi, 2001).

Bradford W. Wright, *Comic Book Nation: The Transformation of Youth Culture in America* (Baltimore & London: The Johns Hopkins University Press, 2001).

Jordan Raphael and Tom Spurgeon, *Stan Lee and The Rise and Fall of the American Comic Book* (Chicago: Chicago Review Press, Inc., 2003).

Daniel Herman, *Silver Age The Second Generation of Comic Book Artists* (Neshannock, Pennsylvania: Hermes Press, 2004).

Gerard Jones, *Men of Tomorrow: Geeks, Gangsters, and the Birth of the Comic Book* (New York: Basic Books, A Member of the Perseus Books Group, 2004).

Gina Misiroglu, ed. with David A. Roach, *The Superhero Book: The Ultimate Encyclopedia of Comic-Book Icons and Hollywood Heroes* (Detroit: Visible Ink Press, 2004).

Jerry Robinson, Michael Chabon, and Jules Feiffer, *Zap! Pow! Bam! Superhero The Golden Age of Comic Books 1938-1950* (Atlanta: The William Bremen Jewish Heritage Museum, 2004).

John Carlin, et al, *Masters of American Comics* (Los Angeles: Hammer Museum and The Museum of Contemporary Art, Los Angeles, in association with Yale University Press, New Haven and London, 2005).

Dr. Arnold T. Blumberg *Pop Culture with Character: A Look inside Geppi's Entertainment Museum* (Timonium, MD: Gemstone Publishing, Inc., 2006).

Peter Coogan, *Superhero The Secret Origin of a Genre* (Austin: MonkeyBrain Books, 2006).

Danny Fingeroth, *Superman on the Couch: What Superheroes Really Tell Us about Ourselves and Society* (New York and London: The Continuum International Publishing Group, Inc., 2006).

Scott McCloud, *Making Comics: Storytelling Secrets of Comics, Manga and Graphic Novels* (New York: HarperCollins Publishers, Inc.,2006).

Simcha Weinstein, *Up, Up, and Oy Vey! How Jewish History, Culture, and Values Shaped the Comic Book Superhero* (Baltimore: Leviathan Press, 2006).